Here Today, Here Tomorrow

How to hire the right people by asking the right questions

Over 700 position specific questions for sales, management, executive support staff, and executive level positions

By Grant Mazmanian, CPBA, CPVA

© 2016 Grant Mazmanian. All rights reserved. No part of this publication may be reproduced, distributed, or transmitted in any form or by any means, including photocopying, recording, or other electronic or mechanical methods, without the prior written permission of the publisher, except in the case of brief quotations embodied in critical reviews and certain other noncommercial uses permitted by copyright law. For permission requests, write to the publisher

ISBN-13: 978-1530625680

Acknowledgements

Thank you to the following individuals
for their contributions and support:

MaryLou Irrgang, CPBA CPVA
Elena Ruiz, CPBA CPVA
Jackie Savoy, CPA
Gregory Mazmanian

Bridget McCrea

Debra Tremper

About the Author

Grant Mazmanian CPBA, CPVA is the President of Pinnacle Group International, located in Media, Pennsylvania. A businessman and consultant for over 40 years, Grant received his Bachelor's degree cum laude from Villanova University in Organizational Development.

As the owner of several supermarkets in Pennsylvania and New Jersey, Grant developed a system to significantly reduce employee turnover and improve customer service levels and worker productivity in a fiercely competitive market. The system became widely known as the behaviorally-based interviewing process. He decided to devote his time to his passion and created Pinnacle Group International in 1983. Today, Pinnacle works with clients in 15 countries.

Grant developed a process for assessing individuals to determine if the individual is a "fit" for the position and a "fit" for the behavioral requirements of the job. To date, Pinnacle's database contains over 30,000 individuals, thus ensuring a predictive accuracy of 90 percent.

In high demand as a speaker and presenter at conventions and seminars, Grant has been interviewed by *Entrepreneur Magazine* and other leading publications.

This book contains information based on Grant's 30+ years of "hands on" experience and research in interviewing thousands of job candidates and training more than 500 interviewers in his behavior-based approach to employment interviewing.

Pinnacle's goal is to help clients hire individuals who will be happy, successful and productive in their jobs. Grant's methods have significantly lowered turnover, increased employee morale, and improved productivity for his clients.

Foreword

As much as things change in the business world from week to week and year to year, there is one fact that never changes: Talent is the number one asset in every organization. This has always been true. The value of talent is even more important to the changing economy than ever before. Hiring good employees is not only important to business; it's *essential*. It is the only way a small business can gain an edge over their competition and for large corporations to maintain or increase market share.

The most important aspect of the hiring process is also the least understood—the interview. Managers do not have the time to do them. The human resource department is swamped; everyone is busy. For most, interviews are viewed as a necessary evil to get someone hired so they can get back to work. Worse, improperly administered interviews are extremely bad at predicting a candidate's success. Why? It's because no one presents his or her "real self" during an interview. The candidate who positions themselves in the most favorable light wins. As a result, hiring managers fall prey to self-deception (its continually shown that perception bias plays a huge role in interviews). We form decisions quickly about whether we like the candidate, then ask questions and seek information that supports our viewpoint.

So how do you get more adept at hiring solid employees for your organization? What can you do to determine culture and functional fit for your company? Considering how heavily weighted the interview is in our hiring decisions, the key is to glean more information from the candidate. And the only way to do that is to ask questions that are specific to the needs of the position. The standard stock interview questions simply do not work.

Interviews are your chance to save yourself a lot of time and money, so it pays to develop a script of revealing questions and listen intently for the answers. This book will help you find what we call "value added individuals"—those that deliver more than just what the job requires.

We are talking about:
- The senior executive who can turn around a division in 18 months with minimal disruption
- The call center manager who gathers important feedback from the customer service representatives on the phone, and routinely suggests improvements to management
- The salesperson that outsells the competition because he or she provides solutions to the customer's problems
- The cashier who rings you up efficiently, smiles and sincerely wants to know how you are doing
- The production line supervisor who can multi-task, maintain quality and is alert to the needs of their team

Today's consumer is becoming more demanding regarding customer service, the speed of delivery, quality and service. It didn't happen by accident—today's mass merchandisers have progressed each year, raising the bar for every company in America. In 1986, an entrepreneur saw an opportunity to create a new and engaging shopping experience through television broadcast. He named the company QVC to represent its three guiding principles: Quality, Value, and Convenience. These values were created to build trust with consumers, creating lifetime, avid fans. Buy jewelry, blenders, designer handbags, computers, Christmas trees without seeing, touching or trying? Preposterous! QVC countered with "love it or send it back." No questions asked.

Fast-forward 14 years to Amazon, which offers over 275 million products, free shipping (with Prime) and, for a small fee, next day or same day delivery. The ripple effect of Amazon impacts every business, small or large. The question is, how are you going to keep up with your competition? The answer lies in your labor base. In the new economy, there is going to be a perpetual struggle in the marketplace to leverage the value of labor. So how do you go about sourcing, attracting, and selecting the best people? The answer to that question is one of the most important things that you, as an employer or manager, can do.

Getting candidates who are the right "fit" for your company from the beginning sets the stage and gets things moving in the right direction. According to Chairman and CEO, Hal F. Rosenbluth, and Consultant, Diane McFerrin Peters, of Rosenbluth International, the third-largest travel management company in the world, "Most of us choose our spouse with care and rear our children with nurturing and compassionate attention. We tend to select the people who will join our company after one or two interviews.

Now, the selection process for hiring employees for your company can be an ordeal. It takes a systematic and disciplined hiring process. The weak link has always been the interview—and more specifically, the interview questions you ask and how you analyze the responses that the candidate provides. The most overlooked and undervalued factor you need to determine is if the candidate's a "fit" with your organization.

Hiring for a cultural fit is equally as important as the candidate's skills, experience, and knowledge. The expression, "People are hired based on what is on their resume and are fired/let go, or quit because they are not a match for the culture of the organization," is true. The longer employees stay around; the more companies save in hiring and onboarding costs. For instance, the online retailer Zappos offers new, struggling employees $4,000 to quit after a week's work, rather than waste resources to train someone who doesn't fit in with the group.

"These trends are being driven by millennials because they care about culture," says Dan Schawbel, author of Me: 2.0. "Research shows that millennials typically stay at a job for about two years—and they have different priorities. They would rather have meaningful work over more pay, or work for a company that gives back or cares about the environment. They want a culture that is less hierarchical, more flexible and more understanding of differences because millennials are the most diverse generation.

Regardless of fluctuations in the labor market, demand for great people is going to outpace supply for the foreseeable future. And hereafter, in the new economy, there will be a perpetual struggle in the marketplace to leverage the value of labor. How do you go about sourcing, attracting and selecting the best people? If your business isn't hiring in a systematic and structured process, you might as well play resume roulette.

After 30 years of helping companies—from a small, family-owned business to Fortune 500 organizations—hire top-performing people for any industry, one principle has remained constant: Hire once, hire right. This book will give you the knowledge and understanding you need to be able to ask the right questions and determine both a functional and cultural fit.

Grant Mazmanian, President
Pinnacle Group International, Inc.
www.pinnaclegroupusa.com

TABLE OF CONTENTS

Chapter 1: The Basics 1
Preparation for a successful interview. Important chapter to read

Chapter 2: Who is Your Ideal Candidate? 11
Learn how to Identify and Measure Attributes

Chapter 3: Types of Interview Questions 21
Discover the right questions for your interview

Chapter 4: Types of Interviews 25
Structure your interview process

Chapter 5: Behavioral Questions by Category 29
Preparation for a Successful Interview

Chapter 6: Cultural and Functional Fit 43
Understanding the difference

Chapter 7: Starting the Interview 53
Very important components necessary for an effective interview

Chapter 8: Tell Me about a Time When You… 57
Successful open-ended questions designed to draw out

Chapter 9: Straight Talk about Money 63
Understanding the dynamics of salary negotiation

Chapter 10: How Motivated is the Candidate? 69
Identifying the DNA of motivation in a candidate

Chapter 11: Key Leadership Questions to Ask 77
Leadership is an innate skill – discover if the candidate has it

Chapter 12: Hiring Sales Professionals 83
Making difficult hiring decisions easier with the right questions

Chapter 13: Questions for Management **101**
Questions designed to uncover management experience

Chapter 14: Candid Questions **111**
Elicit frank and truthful answers to your questions

Chapter 15: Teamwork Questions **119**
Can the candidate lead or be part of a high performing team?

Chapter 16: Reflective Questions **125**
Go beyond "canned" answers candidates have prepared for

Chapter 17: Your Attitude is Showing **131**
Uncover hostile, angry and difficult people

Chapter 18: Probing Questions **139**
Deepen the conversation with the candidate

Chapter 19: Senior Support Staff **145**
Do they have the "right stuff" to measure up to your standards?

Chapter 20: Closing the Interview **155**
Ending the interview correctly

Chapter 21: Conducting Telephone Interviews **159**
Save time and work efficiently, but do it right

Chapter 22: *Don't* Ask These Questions **163**
Eliminate useless interview questions

Chapter 23: The Top 30 Overused Interview Questions **167**
Candidates have prepared answers to these questions

Chapter 24: Questions the Candidate May Ask **171**
Be prepared to answer questions the candidate may ask you

Chapter 25: Steering Clear of the EEOC **175**
Conduct an interview that complies with the EEOC guidelines

CHAPTER 1
The Basics

The Basics

What does it take to have a successful interview?
Do not skip over this chapter. Many interviewers shoot themselves in the foot without knowing it by not following the rules herein. Below is a compilation of over 30 years of experience.

Excellent Candidates have Options
Highly qualified candidates know they are valuable and will choose their next employer based on the position, company's reputation, salary, benefits and other factors. You need to be aware of the recommendations listed below. They are based on follow-up evaluations with the candidate whether they were hired or not.

First Impressions Count
The candidate will rate the quality of the company by the intake process. The adage "you do not get a second chance to make a good first impression" is certainly applicable in this case. If you are interviewing someone who will be working for you, you will always be remembered by what happened during the interview. You may be a "fair and square" manager, but you may be remembered as a tough guy even though it was your job to be a strong negotiator.

Don't Conduct an Interview
One of the biggest mistakes people make in the interview setting is to conduct it as an adversarial—albeit friendly—meeting. The interviewer is looking for reasons to hire, or not hire a candidate using an, "I ask a question, you give me an answer" context. Do not make that mistake. Situational questions work best, so start your question with, "Tell me about a time when you…" Then, actively listen for their response and create a conversation around it.

Challenge the Candidate

Create a scenario around the biggest challenge for the candidate's target job, and then ask them how they would solve it. Not all problems are predictable, but this is still a useful way to see how the candidate thinks. If it is a complex problem, consider sending your candidate an email a week or so before the interview explaining the problem and asking them to come and present their ideas. This strategy is an excellent way to determine how the candidate can help your business.

Ask Relevant Questions

Do not focus on things that are not important. Your customer service manager needs to be able to be a good, verbal communicator and able to diffuse angry customers easily. But the behind-the-scenes information technology (IT) person does not need to be. The latter needs analytical thinking and problem-solving skills; irrelevant questions are just time-wasters.

Maintain a Two-Way Dialog

Let the candidate ask questions. Ask for them throughout the interview. Do not take offense if the candidate asks you, for instance, how long you have worked with the company or your career path. In fact, welcome these queries. Be as transparent as you can—it is to your benefit. Remember, you represent the company. And if the candidate doesn't have any questions, do not assume that's a bad thing. It may well be that you have explained everything.

Don't Speak, Wait

If you want to get more out of the candidate, pause silently for five seconds after he finishes his last sentence. It may seem uncomfortable at first, but this method works. Job candidates who have been on numerous interviews know the questions they are most likely asked, so their answers are practiced and canned. More often than not, that moment of silence will get them thinking, and they'll start speaking candidly. It's what they say <u>after</u> the canned answer that's most important.

Be Respectful
Make sure you are respectful of their time. Good manners go a long way in making a favorable impression. Start on time and end on time. If you need additional time, say, "Can we go for an additional 15 minutes?"

If you take notes (and you should) tell the candidate, "I hope you don't mind my taking notes. It's the best way I know to make sure I won't forget the important matters we are discussing today." Tell them you will share your notes when you are finished to make sure you got everything right. I can't tell you the positive response I get from sharing my notes. I don't recommend that you record the interview. Many people are intimidated by having their conversation taped, so stick with your notes.

Be Gracious
Consider what's going through the candidate's head and put him or her at ease. Come out of your office to greet them. Introduce them to other employees. Smile often and offer them a bottle of water, coffee or tea. Tell them where the bathrooms are, and be a generous host.

Be Prepared
Top candidates want you to take them seriously. Imagine you already had a well-paying job but were willing to make the leap to your company. If the interviewer were not prepared, would you feel confident in his ability to conduct an important interview? Study resumes and highlight anything interesting about the candidate such as awards, accomplishments, or personal achievements. It demonstrates to the candidate that you have done your "due diligence."

Ask Probing Questions

Too often, interviewers ask a question and then move right on to the next one. Good interviewers will continue the line of questioning because they will learn more by getting into the details of a few experiences than by covering each and every job listed on a resume. Because their job is to get beneath the surface and into the nitty-gritty of how a candidate operates, a good interviewer will ask tons of follow-up questions, such as: "That sounds interesting. How did you approach that? Was it successful? What was the biggest challenge? How did you deal with that? What happened next?"

Take your Temperature Early and Often

Be sure to check in with yourself and see if you are "warming up" to the candidate or "cooling down." The candidate is probably doing the same thing. Do not rely on your "gut" because it's usually wrong. If you use the questions in this book, you should have an excellent "read" on the individual. End the interview early if you are "cooling down" with the candidate. Do not waste time on unqualified candidates.

Follow your Timeline

Allow 45–90 minutes (depending on the position) for each interview. Rarely do interviews require more time than this. The longer the interview goes, the more you will find yourself "bonding" with the candidate.

Stay on Task

During the interview, interviewers commonly ramble about the opportunity, the company, the culture and other job opportunities. While this can be an important part of getting acquainted, it is important to give the candidate ample talk time. The more job-relevant information a company has about the candidate, the more likely they are to base their hiring decision on objective criteria, rather than on incomplete (or possibly biased) impressions. A good rule while interviewing is 80 percent listening and 20 percent talking.

Stay Focused
During the structured section of the interview, many relationship-based interviewers go off-script and deviate into something that more closely resembles a friendly discussion. During the last part of the interview, you should stick to the prepared questions and the scripted follow-up questions. The more meaningful and standardized the information collected from candidates, the less room there is to make decisions based on personal opinion.

Stay Neutral
The biggest mistake an interviewer can make is to judge his or her commonalities with the candidate. As humans, we tend to like people who share our personal preferences and interests, such as music, sports teams, lifestyle choices and other behaviors that are not relevant to the job. Weak candidates will try to dwell on these commonalities. While interviewing, remember that being a fellow hunter or boy scout leader is not related to on-the-job performance. Do not let "being like me" or sharing the same values (no matter how altruistic) unconsciously sway your judgment.

Do Not Get Personal
There is no need to discuss your family, hobbies or your wonderful children before or during the interview. It's normal to discuss your interests, but it's irrelevant and unprofessional during an interview. If you want to discuss the stuffed marlin on the wall, or your your football signed by the winners of the last Super Bowl, do it after the interview.

I once sat through a ghastly interview with a quiet and unassuming executive who was interviewing our candidate of choice to be his assistant. She had excellent credentials, and we were anticipating an acceptance of our offer after the interview. This unassuming executive spent the first 20 minutes (I timed it) of a 60-minute interview showing the woman his prized possessions—pictures of himself with sports stars and "important" politicians. He described each encounter with gusto and enthusiasm. It was an awkward situation, to say the least. The woman received an offer but asked for 24 hours to "think it over." She sent us an email with a polite, "No, thank you." One of my staff contacted her to find out why she declined. Her response? She hated sports, disagreed with his politics and was not willing to work for an egomaniac!

Do Not Mistake Nervousness for a Lack of Ability

Many accomplished individuals just don't interview well; their nervousness doesn't make a great impression. But an awkward interview does not mean a candidate can not do the job. Great communication skills are not an indicator of expertise. When candidates seem nervous or uncomfortable, give them the benefit of the doubt initially. Help them relax. You are the leader, and your job is to get the best from people—even those you have not hired yet. And if the people you interview often seem uncomfortable, take a step back and consider your approach. *You* might be the problem.

Do Not Discuss the Plans for the Company

Many interviewers love their jobs and their company. As a result, they project their enthusiasm to the candidate and envision great things for the future. For example, the interviewer may discuss exciting new products, plans for a stock option plan, available promotions (i.e., when a new branch office opens) and other plans that may happen in the future.

The interviewer may unwittingly create expectations that might not happen. Many people have selective hearing—they do not listen to the "might happen" or "may happen," they hear "will happen." Imagine telling your 7-year-old child that you might take them to Disney World during summer vacation. Do you think the child heard the word "might?"

Here is the bottom line: Never mention potential or pending projects. Describe typical career paths, for example, but only in a general sense. When you do discuss plans, stick to details on approved projects or efforts currently underway. Remember, if you cannot promise it, then do not mention it in the interview.

Be Candid and Upfront

Do not gloss over any negative aspects of the job or the company. In trying to sell the candidate to the company, many interviewers skip over the bad stuff such as reorganization or business is slow in the winter.

The candidate must have a thorough and realistic understanding of the job, organization, and culture—including the great and not so great (e.g., a reorganization or reduction in the workforce during the summer). This gives them the opportunity to opt out now and not feel like they were sold a bill of goods once hired. However, you would be surprised that many of those negative aspects are positives to others. Reorganization? Great—that means plenty of opportunities for advancement! Reduction of staff in the summer? Terrific—I have a boat and would love 3-day weekends!

The same goes for the job. If there are boring aspects of the job, point them out. Explain the position thoroughly. Let the candidate know as much as is practical within a few minutes. Do not hold back on the boring parts of the job or amount of paperwork required. They are part of the job, too.

When employers try to downplay the less attractive aspects of the job—such as boring work or long hours—they end up with employees who do not want to be there.

Maintain a Dialogue, not a Monolog

A good interview is a two-way conversation, not an interrogation. It is important to ensure that job candidates get a good understanding of the job, the culture, and the expectations. There should also be plenty of time for them to ask questions.

Do Not Reveal your Questions to Recruiters

Never share your interview questions with recruiters. While often well-intentioned, recruiters tend to tip off the candidates if given the chance. Their incentives, after all, are based on these people getting hired! Do not tell a recruiter that a candidate couldn't read a balance sheet, for example. Instead, explain that the candidate did not meet the minimum level of technical proficiency.

CHAPTER 2
Who is Your Ideal Candidate?

Who are you looking for?

Before launching your candidate search, know the skills and experience that you are looking to hire. More importantly, identify the attributes that are important. Attributes include optimism, competitiveness, empathy and common sense, just to name a few.

Attributes are innate qualities that are developed rather than learned and that are part of an individual's "DNA." Here are sample attributes for various positions:

Customer Service Representative

Empathy – Able to recognize verbal/nonverbal cues and understand the feelings of others.

Teamwork – Works cooperatively with management and co-workers to achieve department goals.

Customer Service – Anticipates and meets the customer's wants, needs and expectations.

Versatility – Able to "change gears" (situationally) as required by business conditions.

Optimism – Demonstrates a viewpoint that anticipates positive outcomes.

System Orientation – Follows and observes company policy and procedures.

Relatedness – Able to quickly "connect" and interact effectively with different personality styles.

Helpfulness – Ensures the customer's needs get met in a helpful and caring manner.

Resilience – Able to "bounce back" and regain composure after an angry caller.

"C" Level Manager

Opportunity Analysis – Identifies new markets and business opportunities for the company.

Competitive – Takes actions designed to increase market share.

Interpersonal Skills – Able to effectively relate and adapt to different personality styles.

Leading Others – Encourages and motivates staff to fulfill the company's vision and mission.

Delegation – Surrenders control by empowering others – maintains oversight, not micromanagement.

Continuing Education – Stays informed of new technology, management theories, products, etc.

Results Orientation – Holds self and others accountable for measuring and achieving company objectives.

Developing Others – Offers promotion opportunities and provides the support for fulfilling them.

Proactive Thinking – Anticipates problems before they occur and seeks to eliminate their source.

Integrity – Relies upon honesty, virtue and sound business principles to run the business.

Long Range Planning – Evaluates available resources and strategically plans for the future.

Human Resource Management – Understands the need to hire the best person for the position.

Realistic Expectations – Sets appropriate goals for staff based on a sound understanding of their skills.

Software Engineer

System Orientation – Follows and observes the company's processes and procedures.

Learning Curve – Learns and applies new technologies and techniques quickly.

Teamwork – Works effectively and productively with others toward the agreed objectives.

Problem Solving – Utilizes a logical and systematic approach to solving problems.

Accountability – Admits mistakes to the manager and makes an effort to avoid repeating them.

Autonomy – Works effectively and independently without close supervision.

Results Orientation – Works in a manner that ensures completion of a task with the required objectives.

Accuracy – Consistently produces work that is factual and verifiably accurate.

Non-Profit

Sense of Purpose – Mindful of the organization's mission/vision, objectives and goals.

Awareness of Mission – Aligned with the organization's mission/vision.

Teamwork – Works with other departments efficiently and effectively.

Personal Commitment – An individual's desire or "stake" to contribute to the company.

Selflessness – Willingness to do "whatever it takes" to complete projects on time.

Unified Commitment – Works with others to fulfill the organization's objectives.

Results Orientation – Demonstrates a sense of urgency to complete projects or reach goals.

Compassion – Able to feel deep sympathy with a strong desire to alleviate the suffering of another.

Receptionist

Following Directions – Understands and follows instructions without continual oversight.

Optimism – Demonstrates an optimistic viewpoint that anticipates positive outcomes.

Customer Service – Senses the needs of others and responds accordingly.

System Orientation – Follows and maintains the company's policy and procedures.

Flexibility – Able to effectively adapt, change tasks or direction "at will."

Friendliness – Maintains a hospitable and amiable attitude towards customers and co-workers.

Process Orientation – Manages and handles the orderly flow of paperwork.

Mid-Level Manager

Organizational Ability – Manages projects, paperwork and priorities effectively.

Teamwork – Creates a work environment that ensures cooperation and productivity.

Common Sense – Utilizes solutions that are realistic and applicable to the situation.

Interpersonal Skills – Able to effectively relate and speak to different personality styles.

Correcting Others – Addresses and redirects unproductive behavior in a non-confrontational manner.

Respect for Management – Demonstrates behavior that supports management.

Developing Others – Offers promotion opportunities and provides support for fulfilling them.

Opportunity Analysis – Identifies new markets and business opportunities for the company.

Proactive Thinking – Anticipates problems before they occur and seeks to eliminate them at their source.

Integrity – Relies upon honesty, virtue and sound business principles to manage the team.

System Orientation – Monitors the effectiveness of the company's processes and procedures.

Sales

Money Motivation – Measures success by increasing net worth.

Competitiveness – Demanding of self to set and achieve sales goals.

Interpersonal Skills – Able to adapt and relate effectively with different personality styles.

Urgency – Demonstrates/communicates the need for the customer to take action today—not tomorrow.

Professional Selling Skills – Consults and advises rather than "sells" a prospective customer.

Executive Level Tolerance – Sells to dominant and strong personalities without fear or apprehension.

Organizational Skills – Effectively plans and manages appointments, follow-up calls, paperwork, etc.

Product Knowledge – Demonstrates knowledge and application of product.

Call Center Manager

Teamwork – Creates a work environment that supports and encourages cooperation.

Interpersonal Skills – Successfully relates and adapts to different personality styles and behavioral types.

Follow Up / Follow Through – Ensures that tasks and goals get completed promptly.

Delegation – Surrenders control by empowering others – maintains oversight, not micromanagement.

Correcting Others – Addresses and redirects unproductive behavior in a non-confrontational manner.

Emotional Control – Maintains a rational and objective demeanor under stressful situations.

Results Orientation – Sets appropriate goals for staff based on a sound understanding of their skills.

Meeting Planner

Common Sense – Utilizes solutions that are realistic and applicable to the situation.

Interpersonal Skills – Relates and adapts to different personality styles effectively.

Follow Up/Follow Through – Ensures that tasks and plans get completed promptly.

Assertiveness – "Takes charge" when necessary and directs the actions of others.

Interdependency – Seeks help when needed but works well without involvement from management.

Adaptability – Capable of changing direction or tasks "at will" as required by business conditions.

Organizational Ability – Effectively plans and manages projects, paperwork and priorities.

Handling Stress – Remains focused and composed in difficult situations.

Accounting Clerk

Process Orientation – Complies with the company's accounting processes and procedures.

Accuracy – Produces work that is free from errors or omissions.

Problem Solving – Utilizes a logical and systematic approach to solving problems.

Interdependency – Seeks assistance when needed but works well without involvement from management.

Organizational Ability – Effectively manages time, priorities and paperwork.

Teamwork – Works productively with others in the administration, sales and production departments.

Accountability – Admits mistakes to the manager and takes appropriate steps to resolve the source.

Versatility – Adapts or adjusts as required by business conditions.

Line Manager – Technical Products

Leadership / Management – Appropriately uses position and power to accomplish purpose.

Accountability – Responsible and liable for their actions plus and actions of others in their department.

Autonomy – Works effectively and successfully without the need for close supervision.

Delegation – Surrenders control by empowering others—maintains oversight, not micromanagement.

Quality/Attention to Detail – Maintains vigilance in managing the details of product output.

Problem-Solving/Decision-Making – Resolves minor issues, conflicts or problems independently.

Correcting Others – Addresses and redirects unproductive behavior in a non-confrontational manner.

Restaurant Manager

Teamwork – Builds and reinforces cooperation between the "back" and "front" of the house.

Interdependency – Seeks help when needed but works effectively without involvement from management.

Respect for Management – Demonstrates behavior that supports the goals and objectives of management.

Customer Service – Displays a willingness to go the "extra mile" to please the customer.

Organizational Skills – Effectively manages to juggle time, priorities, schedules, and paperwork.

System Orientation – Maintains and supports company policies and procedures.

Correcting Others – Addresses and redirects unproductive behavior in a non-confrontational manner.

Versatility – Adapts or adjusts situationally as required by business conditions.

CHAPTER 3
Types of Interview Questions

Types of Interview Questions

Are you asking the right questions?

Use your pre-determined criteria to form pointed questions that maximize your time with the candidate. Use a list of about 7–12 criteria and develop four questions for each factor that you want to explore. Two questions should be positively worded, meaning that they ask the candidate to speak about something that he or she did well. One question is negatively worded in that it will ask the candidate to think about a time when a mistake was made (and how he or she dealt with it). The last question serves as a backup in case the candidate draws a blank on one of the other questions.

There are many different approaches to creating job interview questions: fact, situational/hypothetical, stress and behavioral.

Fact-based or general questions: "How many years did you work for your previous employer?

Most interviews include questions clarifying information listed on the candidate's resume. Questions that ask about <u>why</u> the candidate wants to pursue a job in a specific field (or with your company) also fall into this category.

Situational or hypothetical questions: "What would you do if you saw a co-worker take home office supplies?" Asking the candidate what he or she would do if placed in a certain situation is a situational question. It is not a bad technique, but a lot of people can answer those questions with, "Of course I would ask my co-worker if he or she has permission to take the supplies."

Stress questions:

"Why would we hire you? You have no experience."

Stress questions intentionally put the candidate in a stressful situation. The goal is to learn how the candidate reacts to stressful confrontation—an important success factor for police officers and customer service representatives. However, asking a question like this can come at the expense of bad rapport. "If being able to tolerate interpersonal confrontation was a success factor, I would prefer to go after examples in their background by using a behavioral question," says Turner, who has been hired to help design interview processes for police officers, firefighters, and paramedics. "I very seldom [ask a stress question]."

Behavioral questions:
"Tell me about a time when you initiated a project that resulted in increased productivity."

The theory behind behavioral interviewing is that past performance is an excellent predictor of future performance. Instead of asking general questions, the interviewer requests specific examples that demonstrate skills. For instance, instead of asking, "Do you have initiative?" the interviewer would ask for an example of a time when the candidate demonstrated initiative. Most behavioral interview questions start with phrases like "tell me about a time" or an adverb such as what, where, why, or when. In actuality, you're not asking someone if they have done something; you're asking them to explain <u>how</u> they have done it. This is an important point because it's difficult to exaggerate or fake this interview.

Because they are expected to generate the most accurate responses, most professional recruiters dedicate the majority of each interview to behavioral questions.

This technique might be difficult when evaluating people who are from other cultures or who have language difficulties. Another challenge is that some people just don't think well on their feet. The latter issue gets resolved by sharing the factors that are important for the job with the candidate before the interview.

CHAPTER 4
Types of Interviews

Types of Interviews

There are many different interview types, methods, and techniques. Each method is designed to provide the interviewer the information he or she needs, and each interview achieves a particular purpose.

Screening Interviews:
Screening interviews clarify or confirm information on the candidate's resume. This method should be used if there is a large applicant pool that needs to be narrowed down to a more manageable number. The purpose is to "weed out" the applicants who are obviously not a good fit. Screening interviews are usually done by telephone and focus on differences between what's on their resume and the job requirements, or to confirm important information such as:

- Salary requirements
- Education information
- Willingness to travel
- Employment gaps

The goal is to create a shortlist of appropriate candidates, who will then continue to the next interview. Remember that the person who is calling the candidate will be their first encounter with your company; it's important to make a good first impression. The person calling the candidate must be polite, friendly, appreciative of the candidate's time, and able to answer his or her questions.

Telephone Interviews
A phone interview is a cost-effective way to screen candidates. Consider it a pre-interview that covers the important aspects of the position. The interview should last no longer than 30 minutes—enough to ascertain the candidate's continued interest, ask additional qualification ques-

tions and answer questions from the candidate. Phone interviews are a second level of identifying and recruiting candidates for employment. This is the second "screen" that the candidate goes through.

On-Site Interviews:
Also known as a one-on-one interview, this is the most common interviewing method, and it involves a meeting with the interviewer and candidate at the company's offices. In addition to the official "interview," the candidate gets to meet his or her manager, tour the office, see his or her future desk or cubicle, and meet some co-workers. Depending on the position, it may be a single or multiple interview process.

Panel Interviews:
An increasing number of companies are using group interviews to screen job applicants. This change could be attributed to the desire to reduce turnover and the fact that teamwork is becoming more critical in the workplace. The easiest way to explain it is that two heads are almost always better than one. When there is more than one person doing the interviewing, the chances of making a poor hiring decision can be minimized.

Sometimes the employer will have a "selection committee" or include multiple people in the interview for another reason. The panel interview is also very important when the candidate will be working for multiple managers. The team may want to conduct a "panel interview" in which several people will interview you at the same time.

Serial Interviews:
In a serial interview, the candidate will meet with several people throughout the day, usually back-to-back. One person will interview the candidate and then send him or her to the next person, and so on throughout the day. Serial interviews are physically and mentally tiring because they often consume the entire day. Executive level positions

are most appropriate for serial interviews, but there are other situations when they are also appropriate.

Lunch Interviews

Sometimes it may be advantageous to invite the candidate to an interview over lunch or dinner. Such meetings tend to be unstructured, informal and relaxed. They are also a valuable source of information when learning about candidates' social skills and manners (especially if they will be meeting with clients on a regular basis at a restaurant). People still judge others by their manners. Although they don't need to know Emily Post's rules of etiquette, basic table manners are required.

Group Interviews

The key difference between individual interviews and group interviews is obvious. By interviewing several candidates at once—or even using multiple interviewees—the competition amongst those candidates will heat up. The interviewer will ask questions of no one in particular in hopes that a "leader" will emerge. This type of interview presents a unique view of each applicant in a pressurized environment. After 15 minutes, the entire group stratifies into different behavioral groups. A candidate who speaks confidently without being overbearing, for example, may take the lead. If nothing else, it makes for a lively interview!

CHAPTER 5
Behavioral Questions by Category

Behavioral Questions by Category

MOTIVATION

1. Are you more of a visionary, or more of a fulfillment person? Give me a few examples.

2. What drives you every day? What gets you excited or motivated?

3. What is your pace at work? Are you a slow, moderate or fast worker?

4. Describe a complex situation that became a learning experience. How did you go about learning? Did you enjoy this process? What was the outcome?

5. Do you like facing concrete, short-term challenges; or do you enjoy conceptual, abstract long-term challenges?

GOAL SETTING

1. Give me an example of an important career goal that you set for yourself and tell me how you reached it. What obstacles did you encounter? How did you overcome them?

2. Have you ever found it necessary to sacrifice personal plans for your professional responsibilities? Give me an example.

BEHAVIORAL QUESTIONS BY CATEGORY

3. How have you gone about setting short-term goals and long-term goals for yourself or your team? What steps did you take along the way to keep yourself accountable?

4. How do you set goals for yourself? How do you keep track of your progress?

5. What was the biggest goal you ever set for yourself? What was the outcome?

DECISION MAKING

1. Tell me about a time when you had to make a decision without having all of the necessary information. How did you handle it?

2. Give me an example of a time when you had to come to a decision quickly. What obstacles did you face?

3. What is the most difficult decision you've ever had to make at work? How did you arrive at your decision? What was the result?

4. Give me an example of a business decision you made that you ultimately regretted. What happened?

5. How much information do you need to make a decision? Give me an example.

ATTENTION TO DETAIL

1. What process do you use to confirm that you have the right details for a customer?

2. Give me an example of a time you discovered an error that been overlooked by a colleague. What did you do? What was the outcome?

3. Tell me about a time when you were confused by a customer's request. What steps did you take to clarify the issue?

4. How do you maintain accuracy during a hectic day/week?

5. When you give your manager a report, what steps did you do to make sure it was accurate and complete?

CLIENT FOCUS / CUSTOMER ORIENTATION

1. When have you had to deal with an irate customer? What did you do? How did the situation end up?

2. Tell me about a time you have "inherited" a customer. What steps did you take to establish rapport with them? What did you do to gain their trust?

3. How have you handled a situation in the past where your client has "moved the goalposts?"

4. Give an example of a time when you went well out of your way to ensure a customer received the best possible service from your organization. What was their reaction?

5. When have you ever gone out on a limb to defend a customer? What happened?

COMMUNICATION

1. When have you had to present to a group of people with little or no preparation? What obstacles did you face? How did you handle them?

2. Have you ever had to "sell" an idea to your co-workers? How did you do it?

3. Give me an example of a time when you were able to communicate successfully with another person even when that individual may not have personally liked you (or vice versa).

4. What obstacles or difficulties have you faced in communicating your ideas to a manager?

5. Tell me about a time in which you had to use your written communication skills to get an important point across.

ANALYTICAL SKILLS / PROBLEM-SOLVING

1. Describe the project or situation that best demonstrates your analytical abilities. What was your role?

2. Tell me about a time when you had to analyze information and make a recommendation. What thought process did you use? Was the recommendation accepted? If not, why?

3. Tell me about a situation where you had to solve a difficult problem. What did you do? What was the outcome? What do you wish you had done differently?

4. What steps do you follow to study a problem before making a decision? Why?

5. Tell me about a time you solved a problem and also prevented it from happening again?

CREATIVITY

1. When was the last time you thought "outside the box?" What did you do? How did you do it? What was the outcome?

2. Tell me about a problem that you've solved in a unique or unusual way. What was the outcome? Were you happy or satisfied with it?

BEHAVIORAL QUESTIONS BY CATEGORY

3. Give me an example of when someone brought you a new idea that was odd or unusual. What did you do?

4. When have you brought an innovative idea into your team? How was it received?

5. Tell me about a time you came up with a solution to a problem that hadn't happened yet?

ADAPTABILITY

1. Tell me about a situation in which you have had to adjust to changes over which you had no control. How did you handle it?

2. Tell me about a time when you had to adjust to a colleague's working style to complete a project or achieve your objectives.

3. Give me an example of how you have juggled multiple projects at the same time. How did you adapt to it? What did you do?

4. Define stress and when do you typically get stressed out?

5. Please give us an example when you set a goal for yourself and experienced stress from it??

GOAL SETTING

1. Give me an example of an important career goal that you set yourself and tell me how you reached it. What obstacles did you encounter? How did you overcome them?

2. Tell me about a professional goal that you set that you did not reach. How did it make you feel?

3. How have you gone about setting short-term goals and long-term goals for yourself or your team? What steps did you take along the way to keep yourself accountable?

4. How do you set goals for yourself and stay on track to reach them?

5. What was the biggest goal you ever set for yourself? What was it? What happened?

INITIATIVE

1. Describe a project or idea (not necessarily your own) that was implemented primarily because of your efforts. What was your role? What was the outcome?

2. Describe a situation in which you recognized a potential problem as an opportunity. What did you do? What was the result? What, if anything, do you wish you had done differently?

3. Tell me about a project you initiated. What did you do? Why? What was the outcome? Were you happy with the result?

4. Tell me about a time when your initiative caused a change to occur.

5. What has been the best idea you have come up with during your professional career?

INTEGRITY/HONESTY

1. Discuss a time when someone challenged your integrity. How did you handle it?

2. Tell me about a time when you experienced a loss for doing the right thing. What happened?

3. Tell me about a business situation when you felt honesty was inappropriate. Why? What did you do?

4. Give a specific example of a policy you conformed to with which you did not agree. Why?

5. Tell me about a time when a customer was not truthful. What did you do?

ABILITY TO HANDLE STRESS

1. What has been the most stressful situation you have ever found yourself in at work? What happened? How did you handle it? What was the outcome?

2. What have you done in the past to manage your stress level with co-workers or your team?

3. How do you prevent stressful situations from occurring?

4. How would you describe positive stress?

5. If you had no other choice but to work in a stressful situation for a long time, how would you handle it?

INTERPERSONAL SKILLS

1. Give an example of when you had to work with someone who was difficult. How/why was this person difficult? How did you handle it? How did the relationship progress?

2. What, in your opinion, are the key ingredients in guiding and maintaining successful business relationships? Give me examples of how you have made this work for you.

3. Give me an example of a time when you were able to communicate successfully with another person even when that individual may not have personally liked you (or vice versa). How did you handle the situation?

4. Tell me about a time when you had to work on a team with someone you had difficulty getting long. What happened?

5. Describe a situation where you had a conflict with another individual, and how you dealt with it. What was the outcome? How did you feel about it?

LEADERSHIP

1. Are you a leader? Give me three examples of your leadership at work.

2. What's the biggest risk you've taken in recent years?

3. What was your greatest leadership achievement in a professional environment? Talk through the steps that you took to reach it.

4. What have been the greatest obstacles you have faced in building/growing a team?

5. What do you and your role models share in common?

PLANNING AND ORGANIZATION/TIME MANAGEMENT

1. Describe a situation that required you to handle multiple tasks at once. How did you handle it? What was the result?

2. How do you prioritize projects and tasks when scheduling your time? Give me some examples.

3. Tell me about a project that you planned. How did your organize and schedule the tasks? Tell me about your action plan.

4. When has a project or event you organized not gone according to plan? What happened? Why? How did you feel?

5. Describe to me a recent goal and the step-by-step process you used to achieve it.

SALES

1. What is your greatest sales-related achievement to date? What steps led to the outcome?

2. Describe a time when you closed a sale with a resistant customer.

3. What was the most stressful professional negotiation you have experienced? How did you handle it?

4. Tell me about a time when you had to persuade a prospect to buy from you over your competition.

5. How many times have you exceeded your sales target? What did you do?

TEAMWORK

1. When you are part of a team that is working exceptionally well, to what do you credit its success?

2. Tell me about a time when you had to work on a team that did not get along. What happened? What role did you take? What was the result?

3. What are your team-player qualities? Please be specific.

4. Tell me about a time when you settled a dispute between team members. How did you go about identifying the issues? What was the result?

5. What have you found to be the difficult part of being a member, not leader, of a team? How did you handle this?

TENACITY / RESILIENCE

1. Tell me about a particular work-related setback you have faced. What happened? How did you deal with it?

2. Have you ever found yourself in a competitive situation professionally? How did you handle it?

3. When have you seen your tenacity or resilience pay off in a professional setting? What was the outcome?

4. Tell me about a time when you had to "go it alone." What happened? How did it turn out?

5. Give me a personal example of "when the going gets tough, the tough get going."

CHAPTER 6
Cultural and Functional Fit

Cultural and Functional Fit

An individual gets hired based on his or her skills, experience, and knowledge. The same individual leaves because he or she is not a good fit for the company's culture. You can achieve an ideal balance between these two extremes—and effectively evaluate for cultural fit—by simply asking the right questions during the interviewing process.

It is important to ask interview questions that assess cultural fit. Company cultures can vary greatly, and not every employee will do well or be content in every culture. For example, an individual who prefers a more formal and traditional workplace will feel uncomfortable in a company whose culture reflects camaraderie, teamwork, and "Casual Fridays" every day. Although this scenario may be obvious, even minor differences can impact an individual's happiness.

The goal of the cultural fit interview is to assess job candidates' personal and social/work styles and preferences to ensure they are a good fit within the hiring organization's culture.

Examples of cultural fit questions include:
> Why do you want to leave your current employer? Describe your ideal work environment.
>
> Explain a work environment or culture in which you would NOT be happy. Describe the behavior and characteristics of the best boss you've ever had. Tell me about your preferred work style.

Functional Fit:
Functional interviews assess a candidate's knowledge, skills and experience for a specific job. Functional fit interviews may also include assessment tests to determine how well someone performs a job in required areas, such as coding skills for IT positions or writing and editing skills for PR jobs.

CULTURAL AND FUNCTIONAL FIT

Examples of functional fit questions include:

For specific job functions:

Sales: Walk me through the most complex sale you've ever made.

Marketing: What are some of the biggest issues you've encountered in product launch plans?

Administrative Assistant: What do you see as the most important skills for success in the role of an administrative assistant?

Database Administrator: Give me an example of your process for troubleshooting problems/issues.

More general questions that help determine functional fit:

1. Describe your current workplace. In what ways is it similar or different from your employment at other companies?

2. What do you enjoy about your current workplace? Why?

3. What do you find most frustrating where you work? Why?

4. What factors are crucial within an organization's work environment and must be present for you to work most effectively?

5. What is the single most important factor that must be present in your work environment for you to be successfully and happily employed?

6. Tell me what you think of when you think of a motivational environment.

7. Describe your preferred relationship with your supervisor or manager regarding direction, oversight, and delegation.

8. Tell me about your preferred work style. Do you like working with a team or independently? What percentage of your time would you allocate to each, given the choice?

9. Please take me through your professional career.

10. Why have you chosen this particular field?

11. Do you have a best friend at work? How do you feel about becoming friends with your co-workers? Is this a wise practice?

12. What do you think differentiates you from the other applicants for this job? Why?

13. Why do you think you'd be a good fit for this job?

14. What do you think about an organization that encourages use of your discretionary energy and effort, to go the extra mile, push harder, spend more time, and do whatever is necessary to get the job done?

15. What aspects of your job do you rate as most critical?

CULTURAL AND FUNCTIONAL FIT

16. How would your co-workers describe your work style and contributions in your former job?

17. When you work with a team, describe your typical role within the group.

18. What are your long-range goals?

19. If we hired you, what are the top three goals you would like to see this company (or department, team, etc.) achieve?

20. What can you do for us that someone else cannot?

21. The average tenure of our employees is 15 years. How will you, as a newly hired employee, become a part of our culture?

22. Have you done your best work yet?

23. What do you like most about this job?

24. When working with people, what is your preferred relationship with these individuals?

25. What aspect of your job is the least appealing?

26. How do you plan your time?

27. What are three reasons for a company's success?

28. What is the title of the person you report to and what are his or her responsibilities?

29. What were the biggest decisions you made in the past six months? How did you go about making them and what alternatives did you consider?

30. Describe a major project where you encountered problems. How did you resolve them and what were the results?

31. Describe one of the best ideas you have ever sold to a peer or supervisor. What were your approach and result?

32. Explain a work environment or culture that would make you unhappy.

33. At work, what obstacles typically stand in the way of completing assignments on time? How do you handle these obstacles?

34. How do you know you are doing a good job?

35. How do you measure performance?

36. Can you recall a time when you were less than pleased with your performance?

37. Can you describe some projects that were a result of your initiative? What prompted you to begin such projects? How did they end up?

38. What qualifications do you have that make you successful in this field?

CULTURAL AND FUNCTIONAL FIT

39. Do you prefer to speak with someone, or send a memo or email? Please explain.

40. Give an example of a situation in which you failed, and how you handled it.

41. What characteristics are the most important in a good manager? How have you displayed these characteristics?

42. Describe the behavior and characteristics of the best boss you've ever had.

43. What two or three accomplishments have given you the most satisfaction in your professional career?

44. Describe one of your leadership roles and tell me why you committed your time to it.

45. Have you been in charge of budgeting, approving expenses, and monitoring departmental progress against financial goals?

46. What suggestions did you make in your last job to cut costs, increase profits, improve morale, increase output, etc.? What results did you get? How did you measure results?

47. What do you wish you had done more of in your last job?

48. What specific strengths did you bring to your last job?

49. Think of a failure that you have experienced during your career. What did you learn from it?

50. Can you think of an example of a lesson you learned from someone else's mistake?

51. What risks did you take in your last few jobs? What were the results of those risks?

52. What languages do you speak?

53. What do you do when you are having trouble solving a problem?

54. What interests you most about this position?

55. Have you ever hired or assisted in hiring anyone? Tell me about it.

56. On what basis do you select a new hire?

57. Describe the people that you hired on your last job. Did they work out? How long did they remain at their jobs?

58. What kind of references do you think your previous employer will give you? Why?

59. If you have complaints about your present employers, and they think so highly of you, why haven't you brought your concerns to their attention?

60. The successful candidate for this position will be working with some highly-trained individuals who have been with the company for a long time. How will you fit in with them?

CULTURAL AND FUNCTIONAL FIT

61. What is the most difficult situation you have faced? How did you handle it?

62. How did your supervisor get the best performance out of you?

63. How do you use deadlines in your work?

64. How would you do this job differently from other people?

65. What personality traits do you think are necessary to succeed in this field?

66. Have you thought about why you might prefer to work with our firm as opposed to one of the other organizations to which you have applied?

67. If you could eliminate one responsibility from your last job, what would it be?

68. After being with the same company for so long, will it be hard to adapt to a new environment?

69. Some people feel that spending so much time at one job demonstrates a lack of initiative. How do you respond to that?

70. What are the advantages of staying at one job a long time?

71. Since you were in the same job for such a long time, you've probably grown very comfortable with it—maybe even a bit stale. How would you cope with a new job in a company such as ours?

72. You've changed jobs quite frequently. How do we know you'll stick around if we hire you?

73. How do you explain the diversity of jobs you've had? How will it be helpful in this position?

74. You've been with your current employer for only a short amount of time. Is this an indication that you'll be moving around a lot throughout your career?

75. If hired, how long are you planning to stay with this company?

76. What are some good strategies for managing unfair criticism?

77. Give me some examples of different approaches you have used when persuading someone to cooperate with you.

78. How do you cope with the inevitable stresses and pressures of your job?

79. Tell me about a decision you made that was based primarily on a customer needs.

80. How would your co-workers describe their relationships with you?

CHAPTER 7
Starting the Interview

Starting the Interview

Clean Up Your Space:
Straighten up your office, conference room, or wherever you plan to meet the candidate. There is nothing worse than having a candidate walk into a conference room where books and paperwork need to be cleared off the table before the interview can start. I've seen this happen and stood by while a client had to clean the room before the candidate came for the appointment.

Dress Appropriately:
First impressions work both ways. You are representing the company, so you want to look your best. Essentially, the interviewee will be making a judgment about your company based on how you present yourself. Wear professional clothing that fits within your company's culture.

Be Polite, Friendly, and Sincere:
Be polite and open. Smile at the candidate and try to make him or her feel comfortable as soon as they walk through the door. By establishing early on that you want to know more about the person, you're likely to get more relevant information out of them. For instance, start by saying how delighted you are to meet the candidate with a smile and a handshake.

Introduce Yourself:
You are your best icebreaker, so spend a few minutes telling the candidate about yourself. It will put him at ease and show that you're human, open and friendly. Discuss your position in the company. If you are the candidate's manager, talk about how many years you worked at the company, why you decided to apply, and why you stayed. If you moved up in the company, tell him about that too.

Slow Down:

You may not know this about yourself, but if you are not in human resources, then you're probably talking too fast. Rapid-fire questions are a sure way to kill the conversation, and may even make your interviewee clam up. Slow the pace of the interview, allow pauses and thinking time, and ask follow-ups if you feel the interviewee has more to say.

State Why You Asked the Individual to Come in for the Interview:

Show that you are genuinely interested in the person as a candidate. Begin by talking about why you brought them in. For example, you could say, "I was interested in the fact that you successfully managed a big project, and that's one of the reasons we invited you to the interview." As a bonus, you can use this time to compliment the person on a recent success or accomplishment.

Provide an Introduction to the Company:

Give some basic information about the job, such as the job duties and the hours that the employee will be expected to work. Offer a salary range right up front. Also, provide some background information on the company itself. Candidates may get companies confused or may be unsure about the specific position. Now is the time to establish the candidate's basic understanding of the job.

Begin with an Easy Question:

You can try something like, "Did you have any trouble finding us?" You want to give the person something easy to help break the ice and ease the tension. You could also ask other questions about how the interviewee got there, such as "How did you find out about this position?"

Pay Attention:

The interviewee can tell if you're not listening and may wind up getting nervous or stumbling over his or her words. Also, if you don't jump in as soon as they have spoken a few words, you give them a proper chance to think through the answer and provide additional details.

Gauge your Questions by Their Answers:

Do not be afraid to change your tactics based on how someone answers your questions. You may need to ask for clarification, tweak a question a bit, or ask for more information overall. For instance, maybe they already mentioned that they had several jobs in your field and listed how they were relevant, which means you can delete any later questions related to that topic. If they say that they pay attention to detail, and if you were planning on asking them how their skills fit the job, you could tweak the question a little by saying, "I heard you say that you are detail-oriented. How do you think that will help you in this position?"

CHAPTER 8

Tell Me About a Time When You…

Tell Me About a Time When You…

Always measure success with two scales—behavior and results. Results are a function of "what" got done, the amount of work, and the quality of that work. Behavior is a function of "how" the results were accomplished. Keep in mind that you, as an interviewer, need to measure the candidate on both scales, as both are equally important. Individuals who produced the desired results but who did it with an "ends justified the means" mentality, is more than likely not be the "win-win" person you are looking to hire.

This derivation of the open-ended question makes most candidates comfortable with sharing information. For example, some applicants find themselves less defensive responding to, "Tell me about a time when you made a mistake" versus the more aggressive, "Have you ever made mistakes?" The latter is severe while the former seems to offer applicants permission to share an experience. Half of your interview questions should be of this type.

Don't judge whether or not you agreed with their answer. In fact, there aren't any "yes or no" or "right or wrong" answers. Expect an in-depth response from the candidate. Remember, to ask questions that are relevant to the position. If the candidate is to work in an environment with weekly deadlines and where urgency is the norm, it would be useful to ask, "Tell me about a time when you were under a lot of pressure to produce results on a tight schedule."

Tell me about a time when you…

1. Anticipated a potential problem and developed a proactive response.

2. Were forced to make an unpopular decision.

TELL ME ABOUT A TIME WHEN YOU...

3. Worked effectively under pressure.

4. Accomplished a major personal goal.

5. Handled a difficult situation with a co-worker.

6. Creatively solved a problem.

7. Were unable to complete a project on time.

8. Made a big mistake.

9. Persuaded team members to do things your way.

10. Prioritized the elements of a complicated project.

11. Had to take an unpopular position.

12. Wrote a program (or report or strategic plan) that was well received.

13. Had to make an important decision based on limited facts.

14. Had to implement an unpopular decision.

15. Were tolerant of someone's opinion that was radically different from your own.

16. Were disappointed in your behavior.

17. Used your political savvy to push a program through to completion.

18. Had to deal with an irate customer.

19. Delegated a project effectively.

20. Overcame a major obstacle.

21. Set your sights too high.

22. Lost (or won) an important contract or sale.

23. Hired (or fired) the wrong person.

24. Thought "outside" the box.

25. Had an important goal that you had set in the past (and tell me how you reached it).

26. Had to think "on your feet" to extricate yourself from a difficult situation.

27. Had to come to a decision relatively quickly.

28. Used good judgment and logic in solving a problem.

29. Were faced with problems or stresses that tested your coping skills.

CHAPTER 9
Straight Talk About Money

Straight Talk About Money

Recruiters, job employment websites, and other sources tell candidates not to ask about money, bonuses, vacations, or benefits.

Candidates want to sell you on their worth before discussing salaries. Getting the money conversation out of the way first addresses the most important part of the interview and allows for a more relaxed conversation between you and the candidate. If your offer is unsatisfactory, you can end the interview and get back to work. More importantly, interviewers tend to "bond" with a qualified candidate 30 minutes into the interview. After that, you lose perspective and tend to give candidates what they ask for.

If you have written a descriptive and comprehensive advertisement, there should be no doubt as to what the candidate's expectations are. He or she is aware of the salary range, duties, and responsibilities and expected results. (Remember, you sent the advertisement to the candidate before the telephone or on-site interview.)

Key Questions to Ask

Question: What are Your Salary Expectations? Straight answer:
"I was making $60,000 at my last job, plus bonuses. Given my knowledge and expertise required for the position, I would be expecting at least a 15–20 percent increase." Although a perfect answer to your question, you will rarely hear this response. Don't allow the candidate to sidestep your question. Every article out there tells candidates not to discuss salary until they have successfully "sold" you on themselves.

Example:
A stock answer from CareerBuilder.com:
"It would be very difficult for me to compare my last salary with this position for various reasons—primarily because I don't have enough information about your whole package. I'm sure we can discuss this subject and your entire package by the end of this interview."

Another stock answer from CareerBuilder.com:
"That would be like comparing two jobs that are entirely different in responsibilities and the base and bonus structure. I would be more interested in hearing what the package you offer is before I compare the two jobs. I hope we can postpone this subject until we both have more information to discuss salary and benefits comparisons."

Your response:
"It would not make sense to go forward without knowing your salary expectations. If they are higher than we can offer you, it does not make sense to continue. Your answer does not compromise what we can pay you. I am prepared to negotiate a final offer with you based on your experience and what you can bring to the company." Note: At this point, do not say anything more. Wait until the candidate answers. It may feel awkward, but it works every time.

Offer a salary range

A salary range opens up room for negotiations. Saying "the job pays $60,000 a year" invites a dead-end conversation or a "Mexican stand-off." The objective is to achieve a "win-win" outcome where the candidate feels they have will be compensated fairly.

Money Questions

1. What benefits are important to you?

2. Tell me about the salary range you are seeking

3. Can you recount your salary history for your past two jobs?

4. What salary are you making now?

5. How much did you make at your last job?

6. What salary do you expect to make? How do you base that amount?

7. What benefits package did you receive?

8. What value did you provide to your company and what can we expect from you?

9. Would you expect reviews of your performance tied to salary increases?

10. In your opinion, how much do you think a job like this should pay?

11. Tell me how your experience translates to a fair salary.

12. Why do you think you are worth that?

13. What would be the best way to evaluate your performance?

14. How much money do you want to be making five years from now?

15. Would you be willing to start at a lower salary with an increase upon a successful 30-, 60, or 90-day review?

16. Think about your last raise. Did you consider it reflective of your contribution to the company?

17. Would you be open to a base salary plus a performance bonus?

18. The salary you are asking for is near the top of the range for this job. Why should we pay you this much?

19. Did you ever have a time when you did not receive a raise equal to your expectations? What happened?

20. Would you accept a commission-based compensation plan?

21. Why are you not making more money at this point in your career?

22. On what criteria do you believe you should be evaluated and compensated?

23. How important are stock options or deferred payment plans to you?

24. Would a matching 401(K) be of interest to you?

25. How else can we compensate you besides money?

CHAPTER 10

How Motivated is the Candidate?

How Motivated is the Candidate?

Motivation is one of the most valued attributes to look for in a candidate, and it is especially important in management. But how do you spot true motivation during a job interview? Other values clearly motivate some candidates more than money. Individuals in the airline industry, for example, may enjoy technical challenges, the opportunity to learn new skills, the chance to work with a particular individual, or the opportunity to travel at reduced rates. Finding the candidate's motivation point(s) is very important, especially given the fact that some candidates are unclear about their motivations themselves.

When you consider the answers your candidates supply to motivation related questions, their motivations become that much clearer. Your goal should be to understand the work environment that is most motivating for them. You want to determine whether your work environment and the co-workers will align well with your candidate's motivational needs.

The following questions will help you uncover what motivates your interviewee. A candidate's innate motivation needs to match the behavioral requirements of the job. For example, you do not want to hire a candidate who most enjoys working alone for your customer service position.

HOW MOTIVATED IS THE CANDIDATE?

Questions to ask:

1. Give me three examples of how you are self-motivated.

2. Which do you enjoy more: The feeling of achieving the goal, or the process of trying to reach the goal?

3. Describe your first successful undertaking or achievement.

4. Tell me about a time when the boss was absent, and you had to make a decision.

5. What special responsibilities or assignments have you managed?

6. Tell me about a time when you were in charge, and a crisis occurred. What happened? How did you handle it? What was the outcome?

7. Tell me about an occasion when you chose, for whatever reason, not to finish a particular task. What was the task and why?

8. Have you ever found it necessary to sacrifice personal plans for your professional responsibilities? Give me an example.

9. In your experience, what draws forth your discretionary energy and effort, that willingness each person has, to go the extra mile, push harder, spend more time, do whatever it takes to get the job done?

10. How does your job relate to the overall success of your department and your company?

11. Describe the managerial or supervisory actions and behaviors that you respond to most effectively.

12. How would you define success within your career? By the end of your work life, what has to happen for you to feel as if you had a successful career?

13. What role does your manager or supervisor play in your personal motivation at work?

14. What challenges are you seeking in this position?

15. What actions, behaviors, or workplace events would limit or destroy your workplace motivation?

16. Give me an example of a situation where you had to go above and beyond the call of duty to get something done.

17. What career goals have you set for your life?

18. Describe a work situation where you encouraged the motivation of another person.

19. Observing your co-workers (in your current or a past job), describe what actions, interactions, and encouragement motivated their best performances.

20. You are assigned to participate on a team that has several members who are unmotivated to work hard and contribute. How have you in the past (or would you, if you were to experience it), approached this motivation situation?

HOW MOTIVATED IS THE CANDIDATE?

21. What, in your experience, motivated your best, most successful job performance? Can you give us an example of this motivation in action in the workplace?

22. How do you cope with failure? Please give me an example.

23. What motivates you to put forth your greatest effort?

24. What is the most important aspect of a job for you?

25. Please rank the following from most important to least: job duties, hours, distance from work, pay, work environment.

26. What has been your greatest accomplishment in a work environment and why?

27. How important are external deadlines to your motivation?

28. How do you feel about your present workload?

29. How do you manage your time when things are slow at work?

30. What have you learned from your mistakes?

31. What two or three accomplishments have given you the most satisfaction? Why?

32. How can we best reward you for doing a good job?

33. Why do you think you will be successful in this job?

34. What makes you proud of your work?

35. Tell me about a time when you went "out on a limb" for a job.

36. How do you like to be managed?

37. What kind of supervisor is likely to get the best performance out of you?

38. How important is it for you to learn new skills?

39. What new skills would you like to learn?

40. Do you consider yourself successful? In what way?

41. What is the most important reward you expect out of your career?

42. What is more motivating to you: the salary or the challenge?

43. What do you think determines a person's success in a company?

HOW MOTIVATED IS THE CANDIDATE?

44. Tell me about a project that got you excited to be a part of.

45. What is your definition of success in your chosen career field?

46. You have tried to complete a task and failed many times. How do you motivate yourself to keep going until you completed the task?

47. What is the most important habit one needs to acquire in order to make a person more effective?

48. Tell me about a time when you faced many hurdles while trying to achieve a goal. How did you overcome the hurdles?

49. If you find yourself working with a team that is unmotivated, how do you keep yourself motivated and motivate others?

50. Over time, the job you are doing becomes a routine, and you lose interest. What would you do to retain the interest?

51. What kind of managers bring out your best performance?

52. Can you maintain self-motivation when you experience a setback on the way to achieving your objective? How?

53. Tell me about a time when you willingly volunteered for an assignment. Also, why were you so interested in this specific assignment?

54. Tell me about a hurdle that got in the way of achieving an ambitious goal. How did you go about overcoming it?

55. Tell me about a goal you achieved that seemed unattainable. Why did you keep going on?

56. Describe a work-related goal that you have set for yourself.

57. Tell me about three steps you've taken over the last year to improve yourself, both business-wise and competency wise?

58. Tell me about a time when you and your whole team were discouraged for some reason. What do you do to raise spirits?

CHAPTER 11
Key Leadership Questions to Ask

Leadership Questions

Leaders are the future of all organizations, both large and small. Management and leadership differ in some crucial ways. Management is a hands-on component of leadership and includes responsibilities for planning, organizing, and controlling. Effective leaders, on the other hand, inspire those around them to listen to and follow a vision.

Leadership requires strategic (future based) thinking. Management requires tactical (present based) thinking. Leadership includes the ability to innovate and drive an organization or people towards new ideas and directions. Management includes the fulfillment of a vision or mandate.

The questions in this chapter will focus on exploring and evaluating recognized leadership competencies and assessing whether the candidate has both leadership skills and leadership potential.

It is very important to ask candidates about the times of crisis and when things went wrong. Individuals with leadership attributes speak freely about their failures. You want a leader who learns from his or her mistakes. If they have not made any mistakes, they probably are not leadership material—at least not yet. Remember, you are hiring *experience*, not potential.

1. How would your staff or colleagues describe your leadership style? Please provide some examples.

2. What are the most important values and ethics you demonstrate as a leader? Give me an example of these values and ethics in practice.

3. Are you a natural leader? If so, tell how you are and why.

4. What drives you every day? What gets you out of bed in the morning?

KEY LEADERSHIP QUESTIONS TO ASK

5. Provide some situations that may cause a leader to fail.

6. What major challenges and problems did you face in the past five years? How did you handle them?

7. Tell me about a time when you failed as a leader. What happened? What was the outcome?

8. Describe your first successful undertaking or achievement.

9. Describe another undertaking that was successful. What was the difference between the two?

10. Tell me about your ability to be resilient in the face of failure.

11. What is the biggest risk you have taken in recent years? Was it worth it? Why or why not?

12. Tell me about an innovative solution you developed to a non-traditional problem.

13. Describe a situation in which the pressure to compromise your integrity was very strong.

14. Tell me about a time when the going got tough. How did you rally the staff and build morale?

15. What methods have you used to gain commitment from your team?

16. All leaders have to deal with conflict. Describe a recent disagreement you had to handle.

17. What methods have you used to persuade the team to follow your strategic vision for the organization?

18. How have you encouraged ongoing employee learning and development?

19. What was the most significant change you brought about in an organization?

20. How do you react to failure?

21. What drives you to keep making headway after failure?

22. What do you enjoy more, the feeling of achieving the goal, or the process of trying to reach the goal?

23. What makes someone a leader in his or her field?

24. What can you contribute to this company?

25. How do you evaluate success?

26. How do you handle stress and pressure?

27. What are the three most important attributes a leader should have? How do you mirror up to these attributes?

28. What do you consider the most difficult decisions to make?

KEY LEADERSHIP QUESTIONS TO ASK

29. What do people most often criticize you for?

30. What are your goals over the next five to ten years? How do you plan to achieve those goals?

31. Before you pass away, what's one mark you want to leave on the world? What are the barriers to achieving this right now?

32. What do you and your role models share in common? Where are you different?

33. What was the last argument you had about and what was your position?

34. Describe a complex situation in which you had a lot to learn. How did you engage in learning, and did you enjoy the process?

35. What difficult decisions have you made recently, and would you make this same decision again?

36. Describe your decision-making approach.

37. Do you believe in asking for forgiveness rather than permission?

38. When there is a difference of opinion, how do you deal with it?

39. When was the last time you took a calculated risk and failed? What happened?

CHAPTER 12
Hiring Sales Professionals

Hiring Sales Professionals

Recruiting an effective sales force is a major challenge for most companies. Due to of its impact on the company's bottom line, selecting a sales force is a critical area that requires a lot of attention. In most companies we have worked with, 80 percent of the sales was generated by 20 percent of the sales force. The objective is to benchmark the top 30 percent of sales reps and have a system for determining which candidate meets those standards.

Hiring effective salespeople can be tricky and interviewing them is even more challenging. That is why we have listed 85 questions (plus an additional 74 for a sales managers). By their very nature, these individuals are confident, positive and optimistic about their abilities. Because of this, we suggest using a 6-step interview strategy. Here are five important steps to take:

Create a scorecard

By its very nature, hiring is a subjective process. Things like cultural fit and leadership style are very hard to define quantitatively. However, by quantifying as much of the process as you can, you remove the potential for unrelated variables to impact your new hires. An interview scorecard with objective metrics is a valuable tool, especially if you are interviewing several candidates. In most cases, the last person interviewed gets hired. With a scorecard, you can be objective instead of being subjective. Your scorecard should concentrate on your needs rather than your wants, and should include:

- The length of employment per company.
- Ability to show proof of sales volume.
- On-time to interview.
- Genuine interest to work for the company.
- How many years of selling experience.
- Experience selling in this industry.

- Able to travel 2–3 days each week.
- Verifiable referrals.

Use standardized questions

Too many interviewers shoot from the hip when talking to prospective sales reps or managers. A more effective approach is to use an "apples to apples" comparison approach with a standard set of questions for all candidates. These questions must be specific to the attributes you want a salesman to have. Creating a standard ensures that every candidate gets the same interview and is judged based on the same criteria. It also keeps you focused, with less likelihood of getting sidetracked.

Ask situational questions

A good salesperson should be able to handle the unanticipated and to meet challenges with confidence. For example, ask how he or she would handle a sales situation that is specific to your industry. This maneuver will help to determine if that person understands your sales needs and can address them effectively.

Stay on track

Pay attention to your script, stick to your questions and fill in your scorecard. Most salespeople love to talk and will take over the interview if you let them. Some may do it to avoid your questions. Even the best sales managers admit to doing this.

Determine their interest level

Any candidate serious about applying for a job will research everything they can about your company. The internet yields valuable information on company culture, the management team, maybe even about you. Websites like glassdoor.com, indeed.com, and ratemyboss.com, offer insights that help a candidate make a decision to apply or not. Ask them what they know about the company. If you get a sketchy answer, beware. If they can recite the company mission statement, discuss your products and services and seem to have a good idea about the direction of your company, then you have a serious candidate.

Have a buddy system
Don't ever interview anyone by yourself, especially not a salesperson. Salesmen are relationship-oriented and can "bond" with anyone. Having one of your top salespeople attend the interview with you is ideal, however, even a sales support person can be an invaluable source of feedback. Having an additional staff member attend the interview will also make sure you stick to your questions, monitor the time set aside for the interview and ensure your scorecard gets completed.

Questions to Ask

1. Tell me about a time when you had to persuade a prospect to buy from you instead of your competition.

2. Give me an example of how you took the initiative during a challenging situation.

3. What roadblocks have you encountered from the "gatekeeper" over the phone? Using examples, how do you handle them?

4. Describe the toughest sales challenge you ever faced and how you worked through it.

5. Give me an example of a creative way that you closed a sale.

6. Over the last five years, what notable client retention successes have you had?

7. What have you done to increase sales in your territory?

8. Have you felt you receive adequate compensation for your contributions to the company?

9. Have you often exceeded your sales target? How did you do this?

10. Throughout the last few years, what have been your most notable sales accomplishments?

11. Give me an example of a time you went above and beyond the call of duty.

12. Can you give me an example when you had to handle a disgruntled customer?

13. Tell me about a time when you have had a customer return after going to your competition.

14. How do you handle missing a sales quota?

15. Tell me about an important sale that went on the rocks. How did you weather the storm?

16. Tell me about your most difficult sale. How could you have prevented problems from arising?

17. In sales it can be difficult to get an immediate "yes" from customers. What do you do in these situations?

18. Give me an example of a sales goal you set in the past and the steps you took to achieve it.

19. What sales challenge have you experienced recently? How did you overcome it?

20. What major clients have you closed over the last six months?

21. Tell me about a time when you made a bad first impression but recovered from it.

22. Describe how you determine a customer's needs.

23. Tell me about your training. What have you done to become a better salesperson?

24. Describe to me your step-by-step sales process.

25. Tell me about a time when you made an "impossible" sale.

26. Under what management conditions have you produced your best sales performance?

27. Tell me using examples how you "read" people within the first three minutes.

28. During your time as a salesperson, have you been more successful at servicing existing clients or developing new territories? Please explain.

29. How do you determine if a prospect is interested in your product?

30. When and where in the sales process have you found silence to be a useful tool?

31. What business or social situations make you feel awkward?

32. Would you prefer to sell a big or a small ticket item?

33. When you consider your skills as a professional salesperson, what area concerns you most about your ability to sell? What do you like most about selling?

34. What are the most repetitive tasks of your current job?

35. What bothers you most about sales?

36. What makes you think you can sell consistently?

37. What do you know about our company and its products?

38. What do you like least about the job description?

39. What special characteristics should I consider about you as a person?

40. What do you consider a good day's sales effort?

41. What types of people do you sell to in your current job?

42. Tell me about a sale when your timing was exceptionally good.

43. Tell me about a sale when your timing was bad.

44. Sell me this pen.

45. Tell me how you deal with angry or frustrated customers.

46. Have you ever sold services or products over the phone?

47. What special skills and techniques are required to be successful over the phone?

48. How do you go about establishing a rapport with a stranger on the phone?

49. How many sales calls do you make in a day?

50. How much time do you spend doing paperwork and non-selling activities?

51. How do you organize your day-to-day schedule?

52. How long does it typically take from initial contact to close the sale?

53. What percentage of your sales calls result in the full presentation?

54. Who are your best prospects?

55. Who are your worst prospects?

56. Have you ever broken into a new territory for an employer?

57. How do you turn an occasional buyer into a regular buyer?

58. What was the most important account you have had?

59. What are you most proud of in your ability to develop a territory?

60. Tell me about a time when you exceeded both your quota and your goals.

61. What sales achievement was your biggest accomplishment?

62. How do you rank among your peers?

63. How do you get an impression of potential customers in the first few moments of meeting them?

64. What kind of rewards are most satisfying to you?

65. What type of work atmosphere is most conducive to you?

66. What kind of problems do you have to solve as a salesperson? Do you regard these issues as complex or overwhelming?

67. If you could make one constructive suggestion to management, what would it be?

68. How do you prospect for leads?

69. How do you build rapport with new prospects?

70. What is the most valuable skill you possess as a salesperson?

71. What is the most overrated skill for a salesperson?

72. What were your most successful sales deals and how did you get it?

73. What was your most recent lost sale? What happened? If you could do it over again, what would you do differently?

74. Summarize your last performance review. Do you agree with your manager's assessment?

75. Out of a 40-hour work week, how much time do you typically spend working with prospects? How about working with existing customers?

76. Would you rather pursue new leads or sell additional products to existing customers? Why?

77. Do you prefer to work closely with your sales manager or to work independently? Why?

78. What CRM systems have you used? Which did you like most and least?

79. What are your favorite closing techniques?

80. Why did you apply for this position? What expectations do you have for it?

81. What is your biggest job motivator?

82. Tell me about a time when you were in a slump. How did you get out of it?

83. What qualities are you looking for in your employer? What about in your sales manager?

Additional Questions for the Sales Manager Candidate

1. How long have you been in management?

2. How many people do you currently manage?

3. How do you quantify the results of your job?

4. What have you found to be the most important skills in managing a team?

5. What responsibilities do you hold with other departments?

6. Give me an example when you had to "turn around" an otherwise unmotivated sales team.

7. Give me an example of how you adapt to your sales team's needs.

8. Please explain your hiring process from start to finish.

9. If I were to interview the people who have reported to you in the past, how would they describe your management style?

10. Give me an example, from your past work experiences, about a time when an under-performing employee reported to you. How did you address the situation? Did the employee's performance improve? If not, what did you do next?

11. Rate your management skills on a scale of 1 to 10, with 10 representing excellent management skills. Provide three examples from your past work experiences that demonstrate the accuracy of your selection.

12. Describe the work environment or culture (and it's management style) where you experienced the most success.

13. Describe three components of your philosophy of sales management that demonstrate your values.

14. For you to work most effectively, what factors must be present within an organization?

15. Tell me about a time when you reorganized a department or significantly changed employee work assignments. How did you approach the task? How did the affected employees respond to your actions?

16. One of the sales manager's jobs is to manage performance and perform periodic performance reviews. Tell me how you have managed employee performance in the past. Describe the process you have used for performance feedback.

17. How do you plan an interview?

18. Give me an example of how your sales team adapts to your needs.

19. Tell me about a recent crisis you had to resolve. What happened? What was the outcome?

20. Tell me about a recent time you sales team exceeded its sales target by a wide margin.

21. What types of decisions are beyond your authority as a sales manager?

22. What steps do you normally take to help a new salesperson get settled?

23. How long have you held these management responsibilities in your current job? Did these people report directly and solely to you?

24. How creative should management's role be?

25. What do you perceive the responsibilities of this job to be? How far in advance do you and management typically make specific decisions about directional changes?

26. How would you characterize your management style?

27. How often do you prepare reports?

28. What other departments work with you?

29. How do you schedule projects, assignments, and vacations?

30. How many people have you hired?

31. How have you learned to conduct effective interviews?

32. How do you plan an interview?

33. How do you analyze the training needs of your department or specific individuals?

34. What tasks do you typically delegate?

35. How do you maintain checks and balances on employee performance?

36. What causes the most friction in your department?

37. What types of employees relationships are most productive?

38. What types of employees cause the most problems for you?

39. Tell me about a time when morale was low. What did you do about it?

40. When have you seen proven motivational techniques fail?

41. Tell me some of the ways you have seen other managers demotivate employees.

42. Have you ever become involved in an employee's personal problems?

43. How do you keep the staff aware of company information and activities?

44. Have you ever faced a situation with a staff member who was being less than direct with you about his or her activities?

45. How do you organize and run department meetings?

46. How do you successfully set objectives for your staff?

47. Have you ever had to make unpopular decisions?

48. What are some of the everyday problems you face with your staff?

49. What management situation is personally most difficult for you?

50. What employee behavior angers you the most and why?

51. What do you do when a team member breaks corporate policy?

52. How do you handle poor employee performance?

53. Describe the turnover in your department over the last three years.

54. How many people have you terminated?

55. What steps do you make before deciding to terminate an employee?

56. How do you forecast manpower needs?

57. Have you ever experienced problems with company pay scales when trying to attract new employees?

58. Do you hold budgetary responsibility in your department?

59. What was the most expensive fiscal mistake of your career?

60. How do you take direction?

61. How do you take criticism?

62. Have you had disagreements with previous managers? Please explain.

63. What do you do when you have to make a decision, and no procedure exists?

64. How have past managers extracted the best out of you?

65. How would you describe the best manager you ever had?

66. Tell me about the worst manager you ever had.

67. Tell me about a time when you felt that management had made an emotional rather than logical decision about your work.

68. Have you ever been described as inflexible? Please explain.

69. How does your job relate to the overall goals of the company? How often are you involved in making formal presentations or proposals to management or customers?

70. How do you define the difference between supervision and management?

71. If you could make one constructive suggestion to management, what would it be?

CHAPTER 13
Questions for Management

Questions for Management Candidates

Management interview questions focus on evoking a reaction from a candidate for a certain purpose—to provide a general image of the manager (i.e. the candidate).

Why would the employer want to ask these management questions? Because the answers that the candidate provides present his way of thinking and demonstrate whether he can disentangle himself from a given situation with a good lesson learned. Put simply, it will show how skilled and experienced the person is. These questions also help you understand the manager's performance, verify their ability to consider a complex problem, and gain a clear picture of whether this person is a natural leader or a follower.

Here's a complete list of questions that you can use to assess the ideal manager for your company:

1. How many employees report directly to you in your current job? Describe the responsibilities and activities that these employees have, and that you oversee.

2. How many people have you fired in the last two years? What were the specific reasons?

3. Tell me about the most difficult employee situation you ever had to handle. What did you do about it and what was the result?

4. Tell me about a management mistake that you made in the past. What would you do differently next time?

QUESTIONS FOR MANAGEMENT

5. Even the best managers generate complaints from their employees now and then. What complaints do you think the people you have managed would have about you?

6. As a manager or supervisor, one of your jobs is to provide direction and leadership for a work unit. Describe how you have accomplished this in the past.

7. Give me an example from your past work experiences of a time when you had an underperforming employee reporting to you. How did you address the situation? Did the employee's performance improve? If not, what did you do next?

8. How do you prefer to measure the performance of your department?

9. Walk me through one of more challenging times you had to let someone go. How did you make the decision? How much time went by between the initial concerns and when you ultimately let the person go?

10. Describe the work environment or culture where you experienced the most success.

11. Rate your management skills on a scale of 1 to 10, with 10 representing excellent management skills. Provide three examples from your past work experiences that demonstrate the accuracy of your selected number.

12. Describe three components of your management philosophy that demonstrate what you value and contribute, as an individual, to an organization's culture and work environment.

13. What crucial factors must be present within an organization for you to work most effectively?

14. In some cases, managers feel the need to defend their decisions. Can you describe a time when you changed a stated decision or opinion because you were wrong?

15. Can you describe a time when you pushed too hard for a project to the detriment of that project?

16. How do you cope with the inevitable stresses and pressures a manager faces?

17. What kind of leader are you? Please provide an example.

18. What aspect of this job is the most appealing?

19. What aspect of this job is the least appealing?

20. What aspects of your job do you rate as most critical?

21. How long have you worked as a manager?

QUESTIONS FOR MANAGEMENT

22. If I were to interview the people who have reported to you in the past, how would they describe your management style?

23. If I interviewed your staff members, how would they describe your strengths and weaknesses as a manager and supervisor?

24. Describe the management style that brings out the best in you—your capabilities, ability to contribute, and your daily engagement.

25. Tell me about a time when you reorganized a department or significantly changed employee work assignments. How did you approach the task? How did the affected employees respond to your actions?

26. How have you managed employee performance in the past? Describe the process you have used for performance feedback.

27. When you have entered a new workplace as a manager or supervisor in the past, describe how you have gone about meeting and developing relationships with your new co-workers, supervisors, and reporting staff.

28. Have you ever fired anyone? On what basis did you make that decision?

29. Give me an example of how you motivate your team.

30. Think back to a time when you trained a new employee. Tell me exactly what you did to train that employee and bring the person up to the job's performance standards.

31. Tell me about a tough decision you had to make recently at work. How did you go about making the decision?

32. Think of a good decision you made and one that wasn't so good. What did you do differently in making these decisions?

33. Tell me about an important assignment or task that you delegated. How did you ensure that it got completed successfully?

34. When delegating a recent assignment, describe how you showed your confidence in the person's ability to do the job?

35. Give me an example of when you successfully motivated your staff using incentives or rewards.

36. Describe a time you had to motivate a staff member who was reluctant to take on an assignment.

37. Describe a complicated problem you recently had to deal with on your job. How did you gain a better understanding of that problem?

38. Give me an example of a time you were able to identify and resolve a small problem that had the potential to become a big problem.

39. Describe a time when you provided training or coaching to different staff members on the same tasks.

40. Give me an example of when you had to provide feedback to a staff member who was performing poorly. How did you approach this and what was the outcome?

41. Give me a specific example of when you had to clearly communicate your expectations to a subordinate.

42. Tell me about the steps you took to establish rapport with a new staff member.

43. Talk me through a short-term plan you developed and implemented for your department.

44. What methods have you used to prioritize work assignments?

45. What do you consider to be the most challenging aspect of management?

46. What do you like and dislike about the managerial role?

47. What makes a good manager?

48. What is the most useful piece of criticism you have ever received? Why?

49. What were your organization or department's major goals last year (depending on whether the person was managing the organization or a department)? How did you settle on those? To what extent did you meet them? How did you measure whether or not you met them? Were there any targets that you considered setting, but ultimately rejected?

50. What's an example of a goal you didn't meet? How come? How did you respond to that?

51. What will success look like for you this year? Why is that important? How hard will it be to get there?

52. Tell me about something you accomplished at your past job that someone else in your role probably wouldn't have attempted.

53. How would you describe yourself as a manager?

54. What are some of the most common ways people fail at management?

55. Tell me about an employee who became more successful as a result of your management.

56. What would you do if a subordinate were doing his or her job inefficiently?

57. How do you keep staff members motivated when they are under pressure to complete a project or meet a tight deadline?

QUESTIONS FOR MANAGEMENT

58. How do you delegate tasks to a person on your team and how do you monitor their progress?

59. Give me examples of strategic thinking in past situations as a sales manager.

60. Have you ever challenged or shaken old work methods?

61. How do you make management decisions?

62. How do you reach a decision if you don't have all the facts?

63. How do you usually solve problems?

64. Give me some examples of situations when your improvement initiative made a significant difference.

65. How have you coordinated your team's work to achieve target goals?

66. Describe a time when you had to adapt to change. What was your strategy for handling it?

67. When did you last update your business management education?

68. What are your professional development needs?

69. How do you handle a heavy workload? How do you prioritize day-to-day tasks?

70. How do you handle failures? Provide examples.

71. How do you define your key team members? How do you build and maintain relationships with co-workers, key managers, and customers?

72. What are your influencing tactics?

73. Tell me about a time you had to persuade a difficult person. What did you do? What was the outcome?

74. Are you responsible for performance reviews? Tell me about your procedure.

CHAPTER 14
Candid Questions

Candid Questions

Candid interview questions evoke straightforward and frank answers. When you sense that the candidate feels comfortable, ask one of the questions below. I have found that the best approach for getting the most candid and truthful answer is to preface the question with "I'm interested…" The statement now becomes an inquiry rather than a line of questioning. The candidate feels much more comfortable answering a question that shows sincerity or curiosity. What answer would you, as a candidate, feel more comfortable with—"What are your long-term goals" or "I'm interested in knowing what your long term goals are?"

Sample Preface Statements:

> I'm interested….
>
> I'm interested to know
>
> I'm interested in knowing…. I'm curious….
>
> I'm curious to know….
>
> I'm curious in knowing….
>
> I would like to know…. Could you share with me….
>
> I would appreciate knowing…. I wonder if you could….

Candid Questions

1. What are your long-range goals?

2. How long would it take you to make a meaningful contribution to our company?

3. How long do you see yourself staying with us?

CANDID QUESTIONS

4. How do you feel about leaving all of your perks and seniority to find a new job?

5. Has your manager contributed to your desire to leave your present job? In what way?

6. What do you know about our organization?

7. Why do you want to work for us?

8. Your resume suggests that you may be over-qualified or too experienced for this position. What's your opinion?

9. If you were the CEO of this company what would be the top two things that you would do?

10. What can you do for us that someone else can't?

11. If you stayed with your current company, what would your next move be?

12. What do you find most attractive about this position? What seems least attractive about it?

13. Tell me about the kind of rewards that make you feel adequately recognized for your contributions.

14. How do your work habits change when your boss is out of the office?

15. Why should we hire you?

16. What do you look for in a job?

17. When did you first start thinking about working for another company? What triggered that desire?

18. What will your supervisor's reaction be when you tender your resignation?

19. Have long have you been seriously looking for a new employer?

20. In what ways is your current position satisfying and fulfilling?

21. What are the most negative aspects of your current job?

22. Describe the most significant report or presentation you had to prepare.

23. What is the most important thing you learned from your previous job that you will bring here?

24. What was your most important work-related innovation or contribution?

25. Describe a decision you made that resulted in a failure. What happened and why?

26. How do you organize and plan for major projects? Tell me about a major project you worked on. How did you organize and plan for it?

27. What do you feel are the biggest challenges facing this field? This industry?

CANDID QUESTIONS

28. What do you think it takes to be successful in this position?

29. How have previous jobs equipped you for greater responsibility?

30. What aspects of your current job would you consider to be crucial to the success of the business? Why?

31. What was the least relevant job you have held?

32. What are the biggest pressures of your current job?

33. If there were two things you could change in your current job, what would they be and how would you change them?

34. Why did you leave your last job? (Or, why do you want to leave your present job?)

35. Why do you think you were successful in your last job?

36. How has your last job changed since you have held it?

37. Please describe your last supervisor's management style.

38. If you could make one constructive suggestion to your last (or present) CEO, what would it be?

39. Over the past ten years, where have you been the most successful?

40. Describe to me how your job relates to the department's or company's overall goals.

41. What decisions or judgment calls made the biggest contribution to your company?

42. What were the most important projects you worked on at your last job?

43. Can you give a ratio of the amount of time you worked alone to the amount of time you worked with others?

44. How effectively did your boss handle evaluations?

45. Tell me about a method you developed to accomplish a job. What were its strengths and weaknesses?

46. On average, how many hours a week do you need to get your job done?

47. Can you describe a situation where a crisis occurred, and where you had to quickly shift priorities around your workload?

48. How do you feel about your present workload?

49. What creative or innovative ideas have you developed and implemented?

50. Tell me about a team project that you are particularly proud of and describe your specific contribution.

51. Tell me about a difficult decision you had to make. What made it difficult? What did you learn from it?

CANDID QUESTIONS

52. What was the hardest business or work related decision you ever had to make, and how did you handle it?

53. What are the most difficult aspects of your current job, and how do you approach them?

54. What are some of the basic factors that motivate you at work?

55. What do you look for when you hire people?

56. Have you ever had to fire people? What were the reasons, and how did you handle the situation?

57. What important trends do you see in our industry?

58. Tell me about the rewards that make you feel adequately recognized for your contributions.

59. How could your boss do a better job?

60. What do you think of your current boss?

61. Have you ever had to stifle your normal behavior to get along with someone?

62. How well do you manage high-pressure situations? Give me some examples.

63. What quality or attribute do you feel most contributes to your career success?

64. What personal weakness has caused you the greatest difficulty on the job?

65. Describe the characteristics of a successful manager.

66. Why did you decide to seek a position in this field?

67. Tell me what you know about our company.

CHAPTER 15
Teamwork Questions

Teamwork Questions

Discover the Candidate's Ability to Work Effectively with Others

A well built work team is the most valuable asset a company can possess. A team that works collaboratively is a very strong force that allows the company to take on more work and generate more revenue without having to hire more staff.

If the candidate is going to work on a team or collaborate closely with others, use the questions below to come up with key talking points that reflect the needs of the position. The more specific the question is to the job, the better the chances that the best candidate will rise to the top of your list.

1. When you are part of a team that is working exceptionally well, to what do you credit its success?

2. Give me an example of specific accomplishment you achieved as a participant on a team.

3. Tell me about a time when your team objected to your plan. How did you persuade them to adopt your point of view?

4. Tell me about a positive team experience.

5. What qualities do you have that make you an effective team player?

6. What qualities do you have that make you an effective team leader?

TEAMWORK QUESTIONS

7. Have you been a team leader? Describe your role as a team leader. Tell us about the challenges you faced in trying to resolve issues among team members. What could you have done to be more effective?

8. Can you communicate effectively with different personalities? Please give me a few examples.

9. Describe a project that required input from people at different levels of the organization. How did it go?

10. Describe a disappointing team experience. What could you have done to prevent it?

11. Give me an example of a specific accomplishment you have achieved as a team participant.

12. Tell me about a time when your team made emotional decisions about a project. What happened and how did you handle it?

13. Have you ever had an experience where there were issues or strong disagreement among the team members? What did you do?

14. Describe teamwork. Give me some examples.

15. Describe cooperation. Give me some examples.

16. In your experience, what are the qualities of a good team player?

17. What type of people are the most productive? At work? In business?

18. What types of people do you find difficult?

19. Tell me about a time when you said "no" to a co-worker who asked you to drop everything to help them out.

20. Tell me about a time when a team fell apart. Why did it happen and what did you learn from this?

21. Tell me about a job or project where you had to gather information from many different sources and then synthesize it to solve a business challenge.

22. How do you schedule and commit to quiet time by yourself?

23. How do you operate as a team player?

24. How do you deal with people that have backgrounds and value systems that differ from yours?

25. Do you prefer working with others or alone?

26. What good or bad work habits did you pick up from your first job?

27. How do you know when a team has met its objectives?

28. Describe your approach to evaluating risk.

29. What types of people make you most productive?

TEAMWORK QUESTIONS

30. How do you establish a positive working environment for your team?

31. What is one thing a teammate can say to you that is guaranteed to make you lose confidence in them?

32. How do you get along with superiors?

33. How do you get along with co-workers?

34. Tell me about a time when you had to resolve a serious conflict.

35. How do you get along with people whom you supervise?

36. What are your team-player qualities? Please be specific.

37. What have you learned about guarding against "groupthink?"

38. Have you developed any special techniques for brainstorming?

39. Can you predict an individual's behavior based on an initial reading?

40. Tell me about a specific accomplishment you have achieved as a team participant.

41. Tell me about an occasion when the team objected to your ideas. What did you do to persuade the team of your point of view?

42. As a team leader, how much tolerance do you have for mistakes or false steps? In other words, if a team member wanted to do something in a way you were convinced was a mistake, how would you weigh the team member's learning experience against protecting the project?

43. Have you ever been in a team where people overrule you or won't let you get a word in edgewise? How do you handle it?

44. In any team, there will always be a range of aptitudes. Not only is the spread of talents obvious, but team members are in remarkable agreement about the distribution. Put any ten people in a room and they will sort themselves out from top to bottom in short order. Do you believe it is useful to the organization to formally rank team members?

45. As a member of a team, how do you see your role?

46. As a member of a team, how do you handle a team member who is not pulling his or her weight?

47. Tell me about a time when you were chosen to assign tasks to the team. How did it go? Did you pick the right people for the right task?

48. What have you found to be the difficult part of being a member (not leader), of a team?

CHAPTER 16
Reflective Questions

Chapter 16

Reflective Questions

Make Them Think Before Answering

These questions require thoughtful consideration by the job candidate. Reflective questions are difficult because they force someone to go beyond the rehearsed, prepared responses during the interview. If you get a short answer, press deeper by saying, "Tell me more about that? Why is that? Why did you say that?"

Do not rush through these questions. Always pause for five seconds to give the candidate some time to elaborate.

1. Before you pass away, what is one mark you want to leave on the world? What are the barriers to achieving this goal right now?

2. Under what circumstances have you broken or bent the rules? What was your justification?

3. Do you like to compete? How do you view your rivals?

4. Which do you enjoy more, the feeling of achieving the goal or the process of trying to reach the goal?

5. If you never had to work, where would you spend your time and why?

6. How do you react when someone is hostile towards you?

7. How do you react to failure?

REFLECTIVE QUESTIONS

8. What commonalities do you share with your role models?

9. Where are you different from your role models?

10. Do you believe that some people are natural geniuses, or naturally just more talented in the things for which they have a passion?

11. How do you respond when you see people that claim to be overnight successes do you see them as simply lucky?

12. On a scale of 1 to 10 with 10 being a perfect score, how would you rate your former company? What would make it a 10 (if the candidate rated less than 10)?

13. Who was the manager that impressed you the most? Why?

14. Describe your first successful undertaking or achievement. What made it successful? What mistakes did you make? What did you learn?

15. Who is a major influence in your life? How has this person affected you?

16. Has your tolerance for other people's mistakes increased or decreased over the past five years? Please explain.

17. What have you learned most from your successes? How have they impacted you personally?

18. What have you learned most from your failures? How have they impacted you professionally?

19. What is the unwritten rule your subordinates would say about working with you?

20. How have you benefited from your disappointments?

21. How have you benefited from your successes?

22. Tell me about a time when your manager disagreed with your proposal. How did you handle it? What did you do? What was the outcome?

23. Tell me about a time you disagreed with a subordinate. How did you handle it? What was the outcome?

24. Describe a situation when someone criticized your work or idea. How did you react?

25. Tell me about a time you knew you were right and didn't back down to your manager. What happened? What did you say? What was the outcome?

26. What is your greatest achievement and why?

27. What's the difference between a great manager and a great leader?

28. How would you evaluate your ability to deal with conflict? Give me an example.

REFLECTIVE QUESTIONS

29. Would you say that you easily deal with high-pressure situations?

30. What quality or attribute do you feel will most contribute to your career success?

31. What personal weakness has caused you the greatest difficulty in school or on the job?

32. Why did you decide to seek a position in this field?

33. Which is more important to you, the job itself or your salary?

34. What position would you really want in this company?

35. Would people say you're someone who diligently pursues every single detail, or are you more of a big-picture person?

36. What beliefs or personal values govern your life? Explain a few of them to me.

37. Describe a situation in which the pressure to compromise your integrity was very strong.

CHAPTER 17
Your Attitude is Showing

Your Attitude is Showing

Uncovering Hostile, Angry and difficult people

Hostile employees are a drain on productivity in the workplace because they consume resources that should be invested in operating a profitable business. Hostile employees range from those who are passive-aggressive, to those who can be belligerent or even violent toward their co-workers. The result is a work environment created by a hostile boss or co-worker whose actions, communication, or behavior makes working effectively and productively difficult.

Tom is a manager of a small team of people in a satellite office for a large company. Most of the time he is friendly, smiling, even likeable, but his anger is just below the surface. He manages his staff through his "friendly" form of intimidation. Get on his bad side and you will feel the brunt of his wrath. He is a bully in every sense of the word. Agree with him and all is well. Everyone in the office wishes he would find another job elsewhere, but these types never do. He has his "domain" to rule and independence from corporate - why should he leave? Retirement is their only salvation.

Unfortunately, the workplace is not a democracy. Tom could not be "voted" out of his job. The corporate office was not aware of his behavior because no one dare report him. Your job is to uncover candidates who may have anger issues that will not come out in an interview unless you ask the right questions in this chapter.

There will be times when an employee will experience a wide range of situations and experience an even wider range of emotions. Most employees will get angry, possibly talk to their boss about it or simply let it go. But there are also many emotionally immature people, like Tom, out there. They internalize their anger and focus on the negative. The result? They become hostile, passive-aggressive, and a problem for their co-workers and management.

And it all started with the question, "What happened?" which is the goal of the questions in this chapter. When I am consulting onsite, I frequently hear about people who have "bad attitudes." If I get a chance to speak to them, I ask, "What happened?" "There was a time when you were a real team player, but it doesn't seem that way now." They ultimately get to the "what happened." And, inside there is a five-year-old boy or girl stamping their feet and yelling "that's not fair, that's not fair!" Of course, it wasn't fair, but life is not always fair. But try to tell that to 5-year-old "adult" who collected evidence making a mountain out of a normally small disappointment.

The underlying problem arises from childhood and surfaces as an adult be it an unfair decision, unfair expectation, unfair raise—in a word—"Unfair." Here are some examples:

- Someone promoted over the employee because of political/family/gender reasons.
- The employee promised a raise, promotion or important project, and it did not happen.
- Other people who "suck up" to the boss and get the plum assignments.
- Expectations set by the manager were too high—almost impossible to reach—and the person could not win.
- Supervisor was a micromanager and frequently criticized the employee.
- The employee felt better qualified and skilled than his supervisor.
- Another employee doing the same job is earning more money.
- The list goes on...

You will be surprised how many candidates who feel victimized will open up as long as you ask the question in a neutral and unbiased manner. They usually have a story that they believe the interviewer will understand. Listen to situations where the candidate felt helpless or could not do anything to remedy their situation. If you pick up a distinct sense of a problem person, ask a few more of the questions in this chapter.

The interview is only one part of the process to weed out individuals who are hostile. Pinnacle Group provides pre-employment behavioral assessments that help identify negative behaviors that may not be revealed during the interview process. A background check is also an excellent source of information about the candidate. Traffic citations such as speeding tickets or DUIs (especially if they are recent) are a good indicator of character. Crimes resulting in misdemeanors or felonies show another side of the individual. Poor credit may signal opposition to authority. Some states will not allow background checks unless it is relevant to the position. Check with HR or call our office for more information. Do not expect a former employer to tell you anything negative about a candidate for fear of a lawsuit.

The following interview questions can help weed out potentially problematic candidates.

1. It's human nature to feel a wide range of emotions at work. Tell me about a time when you got irritated at work. What happened? What was the outcome?

2. Have you ever had an extremely annoying co-worker? How did you deal with it?

3. Ever been criticized by your boss in front of others? What happened? What did you do about it?

4. Tell me about a time you almost "lost it" at work. What happened? How did you deal with it?

5. How do you deal with co-workers or supervisors who do not show you proper respect?

6. What situations make you angry?

7. Have you ever had a situation where someone took the credit for your idea? What happened? How did you feel?

8. Tell me about a time where you had to deal with a manager who made an unfair remark to you. What happened? What was the outcome?

9. Tell me about the worst boss you ever had. How did you feel about him or her? What behaviors prompted you to tell me about this person?

10. Have you ever had to cope with an uncooperative co-worker? What did they do?

11. What types of people annoy you?

12. When was the last time you got frustrated at work? What happened? How do you handle it?

13. Were you ever promised a raise, promotion or important project, and it did not happen? How did you feel? How did you deal with it?

14. Tell me about a time when you were told to do something you felt was wrong or incorrect but still had to do it.

15. Did you ever have a manager who had unrealistic expectations of your performance or the performance of others? How did you deal with it?

16. Have you ever had a boss who kept changing project priorities without consulting anyone?

17. Have you ever had a boss who frequently criticized you or other people? Tell me about it.

18. Did you ever think that you had more experience and were better qualified than your boss? Tell me about it.

19. Ever had a co-worker who was doing the same job and who made more money than you? Why did this happen? How did you feel about it?

20. Tell me about a time when you were unreasonably criticized. What were the circumstances? How did you handle it?

21. Have you ever had to work with a manager who was unfair to you, or who was just plain hard to accommodate?

22. How would you describe a difficult manager?

23. Have you ever been in a dispute with a supervisor? What was it about and how was it resolved?

24. Give me an example of a time when you experienced rejection at work. What happened? How did you feel?

25. Everyone has pet peeves at work. What are yours?

26. What problems do you have getting along with others?

27. What are some of the things your supervisor did that you disliked?

28. Were you ever fired from a job for a reason that seemed unjustified?

29. What worries you at work?

30. Tell me about a time when you were given a project and did not have enough time to complete it.

31. What do you do when you need to make a decision when no procedure existed?

32. If your supervisor were to fire you, how should it be handled?

CHAPTER 18
Probing Questions

Probing Questions

Discover Past Performance and Challenges

How an applicant successfully handled a specific situation in the past is a likely indicator of how he or she will approach a similar situation in the future. If an applicant has been able to adapt to change quickly in the past, for example, then he will probably be comfortable with the change in the future. If an applicant has demonstrated a good track record in sales, she will likely continue to be an effective salesperson in the future.

The questions in this section are designed to elicit subjective responses, such as how they felt, what motivated them, or why they chose a particular strategy for solving a problem. As the interviewer, you must understand the requirements of the new position and present the applicant with questions that will reveal his or her past functioning in specific areas. Here are some talking points to use:

1. Tell me about the importance of your job (not just the work you performed, but also the importance of doing that work).

2. What do you think it takes to be successful in your career?

3. Do you have the qualifications and personal characteristics necessary for success in this position? Why?

4. Based on what you know about our company, how do you plan to be successful here?

5. What do your past two jobs have in common with each other?

PROBING QUESTIONS

6. How do your past two jobs differ from each other?

7. Can you describe a situation where a crisis occurred, and where you had to shift priorities and workload quickly? What happened? What was the result?

8. Have you held other positions like the one you are applying for today? If yes, describe how you expect the positions to be the same.

9. What aspects of your past job were important to your employer?

10. Why did you leave your last job? What prompted you to seek employment in another company?

11. Did your last job contribute significantly to your department? How so?

12. What factors motivate you at work?

13. What factors demotivate you at work?

14. Describe the ideal setting at a job. How do you see it?

15. What was your most important work-related innovation or contribution?

16. Why have you chosen to interview with this company?

17. Do you expect to change careers sometime in the future?

18. What specific goals have you established for your career?

19. What do you think it takes to be successful in this position?

20. How have previous jobs helped you to take on higher accountabilities?

21. What was the least relevant job you have held?

22. How long will it take for you to be "up to speed" with the requirements of this position? How can we help?

23. What did you enjoy most about your last job?

24. What did you enjoy least about your last job?

25. What were (or are) the biggest pressures on your last job?

26. What do you feel are the biggest challenges facing this industry?

27. What is the most important thing you learned from your previous experience that you will bring to this job?

28. If there were two things you could change in your last job, what would they be?

29. How has your last job changed since you've held it?

PROBING QUESTIONS

30. Did the priorities of your job change over time? Tell me about it.

31. If you could make one constructive suggestion to your last CEO, what would it be?

32. Of all the work you have done, where have you been the most successful?

33. Describe how your job relates to the overall goals of your department or the company as a whole.

34. What are the most mundane tasks in your job?

35. What were the most important projects you worked on at your last job?

36. Can you give a ratio of the amount of time you worked alone to the amount of time you worked with others?

37. How fair or relevant were your performance evaluations?

38. Tell me about a system or procedure you developed to accomplish a job. What did it produce? How well did it work?

39. How many hours a week, on average, do you need to get your job done?

40. How do you feel about your present workload?

41. In what ways has your manager contributed to your decision to leave your present job?

42. What will your supervisor's reaction be when you tender your resignation?

43. Describe the most significant report or presentation you had to prepare.

44. What creative or innovative idea have you developed and implemented?

45. Tell me about a team project of which you are particularly proud. What was your specific contribution?

46. What was the hardest decision you ever had to make, and how did you handle it?

47. What are the most difficult aspects of your current job, and how do you approach them?

48. What caused you the most problems in executing your tasks?

49. How do you intend to learn what you need to know to perform well in this job?

CHAPTER 19
Senior Support Staff

Senior Support Staff

Senior support staff (don't call them executive assistants) are a crucial aspect of a successful business, yet many times they get hired without the due diligence the position requires.

I received a call from a vice president of a corporate division who was experiencing a high executive assistant turnover rate. The job was an important one; the assistant would be providing support services for an executive in the company. "How high was the turnover?" was my question. The answer? Four in the last year and one of them lasted just four months. The problem? The job required someone who could work in an office where urgency was the norm, and where the individual had to multitask and still maintain accuracy, respond quickly by changing "gears" when necessary, and remain gracious and calm when talking to the client.

This vice president knew he had hired the wrong people, but he said, "But they seemed capable and competent during the interview." He shared his interview question list and notes from the past two hires with me. Here are several questions he asked along with more detailed, probing questions from this book.

Can you multitask?
> *Tell me how you deal with priorities when they change quickly. Please give me an example.*

Can you make quick decisions?
> *Give an example of a time when you had to come to a decision relatively quickly.*

Can you work under pressure?
> *Tell me about a time you were in a high-stress situation. What happened? How did you handle it?*

SENIOR SUPPORT STAFF

Can you work independently?
> *Tell me about a time when you had to work independently on an important project with little supervision.*

Questions to ask senior support staff:

1. This position requires you to juggle multiple tasks and still maintain accuracy. Can you give me some examples of how you manage to do that in your current job?

2. What is your comfort level in working with people in senior managerial levels and do you think you can manage the responsibility that comes with the role?

3. Describe any innovations you successfully made in your last job to improve efficiency.

4. Give me an example how you stay focused when things are chaotic.

5. Explain to me how you manage to be effective when under pressure.

6. Tell me about a time you were in a high-stress situation. What happened? How did you handle it?

7. Give me an example of how you prevented a problem from happening again.

8. Give an example of a time when you had to come to a decision relatively quickly.

9. What types of decisions do you make rapidly? What types takes more time? Give examples.

10. Tell me about a situation when you had to speak up (i.e., be assertive) to get an important point across.

11. Describe a time when you anticipated potential problems and developed preventive measures.

12. Tell me about a time you needed to assert yourself. What happened? What did you do?

13. Tell me how you deal with fast-changing priorities. Please give me an example.

14. How do you ensure that your written work is accurate and correct to the best of your knowledge? Do you use a routine method to manage this?

15. What steps would you take to prompt your boss to act on a task (e.g., sign a contract)?

16. Describe in detail the busiest job you have ever experienced.

17. Can you give me an example of the sort of deadlines you've had to meet?

18. What is your system for efficiently organizing meetings, planning travel schedules, and preparing for bids and proposals?

19. In your present company, how is your typical day structured?

20. How do you prioritize your work?

21. Describe the best manager you've ever had.

22. Give me a description of an ideal manager.

23. How do you get people to cooperate with you? Please give examples.

24. What motivates you at work?

25. What demotivates you at work?

26. What conditions would cause you to feel uncomfortable at work?

27. Can you explain to me, using examples from your current or past jobs, how you perform in a fast-paced environment where specific guidance might not always be available?

28. How do you clarify unclear assignments?

29. How does your work experience equip you for this job?

30. What reports did you have to compose, format, check and distribute?

31. What types of data management systems have you used?

32. How did you ensure that data was kept current, and that is was accurately completed? How did you ensure efficient retrieval of information? What information were you responsible for processing?

33. What sort of information did you have to keep confidential in your last clerical job?

34. What experience do you have with setting up meetings?

35. How did you organize venues, inform participants, organize documentation, and set up the meeting room? Were you also responsible for taking and distributing minutes?

36. Were you responsible for coordinating any events, projects or programs? Give examples.

37. What do you consider the most important qualities for this position?

38. Tell us a little more about yourself as a person and give us an insight into what made you choose your career path.

39. What organizational methods do you use to maintain proper records of management reports and to ensure that there is no miscommunication or loss of information?

40. How do you ensure that there is never any breach of confidentiality on your side?

41. Describe your computer skills. Are you proficient with the different office applications integral to your job profile?

42. What do you expect from our company?

43. Tell us about your most recent experience as an executive assistant.

44. Do you have a good working knowledge of Microsoft Office? Explain your use of PowerPoint to create a presentation.

45. Have you been directly involved in making travel arrangements and preparing expense reports?

46. Do you consider yourself to be a single- or multi-tasker? How do you handle being pulled in two or more directions at once?

47. How would you respond to a co-worker who asked you for confidential information (or information that you weren't sure was confidential or not)?

48. In this position, you will be required to guide other administrative support personnel. What characteristics do bring to the table in this regard?

49. What work-related situations do you find the most frustrating?

50. What is missing from (or, is a part of) your present job that you would like to see in this one?

51. This is a hectic business. Everyone is always under pressure to get their jobs done on time in the face of sudden changes in the scope of a job, emergencies, mistakes, etc. Getting everyone's cooperation in getting paperwork to you on time is a challenge. Has this ever happened to you? Can you give me an example in a current (or past) job of how you handled it?

52. How do you schedule your time? Set priorities? How do you handle doing five things at once?

53. Have you had to "sell" an idea to your co-workers or boss? How did you do it? Did they "buy" it?

54. Tell me about a time when you solved a problem using an "out of the box" solution.

55. Describe a situation when you fixed a problem that no one else could solve.

56. Give me an example of how you stopped a recurring problem.

57. Give an example of a time when you had to come to a decision relatively quickly.

58. Tell me about a difficult decision you made during the last year.

59. Tell me a little about what you do (or did) on a typical day in your past or previous jobs as an accounting manager. What are (were) your duties and responsibilities, what are (were) you accountable for?

SENIOR SUPPORT STAFF

60. Why would you miss a day of work?

61. Why would you call in late to work?

62. How many days of work did you miss last year?

CHAPTER 20
Closing the Interview

Closing the Interview

Questions to Draw the Interview to a Close

How you close the interview is just as important as how you start it. When the interview is over, or when you have all the information you think you need to make a decision, end the interview. Thank the candidate for taking the time to come in. Summarize the key points of the discussion to verify accuracy. Finally, give the candidate the opportunity to ask questions. The quality and relevance of these questions will reveal even more about the applicant's qualifications.

Review the next steps in the interview process. If you think the candidate is qualified let her know that she's considered for the position. Don't leave the candidate hanging by saying, "We'll get back to you." Instead, say, "Someone will get back to you in two days." Work fast. In many instances, I've seen great candidates take another position because they didn't get any feedback from the interviewer or because they hadn't heard back promptly.

Be gracious when finished and be sincere when thanking them for coming in. It may sound foolish or awkward to thank them—let's face it, they should be thanking *you* for the opportunity—but it is a nice gesture. It makes them feel important and appreciated. It just might make all the difference in the world for that talented person to choose your company over another opportunity.

When we asked candidates to critique the interview they just completed, almost all were impressed with the opening and closing of the interview. In many instances, candidates who didn't get the job spoke highly of the company and recommended others to apply for an open position at the firm. When you ask, "How did you find out about this position?" And when they reply, "A friend of mine who applied here in the past recommended that I apply for the position," you know you completed an excellent interview.

CLOSING THE INTERVIEW

Use these questions to close the interview:

1. Well, based on what we have discussed, how do *you* feel about this job?
2. Do you have any more questions?
3. Is there anything else we haven't covered?
4. Is there anything else I should know about you?
5. I've interviewed several very good candidates, and I will admit that you are one of them. What single message would you like me to remember that will convince me that you are the one we should hire?
6. How do you think you performed during this interview?
7. What have you been able to learn about our firm and our management team?
8. If I offered you the position today would you accept?
9. Do you have a clear and accurate understanding of the position?
10. When can you start?
11. May we contact your present employer and references?

12. Is there anything you'd like to know about the job that would help you perform better than anyone else could?

13. If there were one reason we should select you over the other applicants, what would that be?

14. Our time is about up. Is there a final point you would like to make?

15. Do you want this job? Then why, throughout our entire discussion, have you not asked for it?

CHAPTER 21
Conducting Telephone Interviews

Conducting Telephone Interviews

Most of our clients are using telephone interviews. They found that to be an excellent way to evaluate a candidate without having to block time out of their busy schedules. Candidates have time issues as well. Individuals who are currently employed, for example, will greatly appreciate being able to interview via phone on their lunch breaks.

There's a certain process to interviewing via phone. For starters, follow a 5-20-5 rule—that is spend 5 minutes talking about the company and the job opportunity background, 20 minutes asking questions, and 5 minutes answering the candidate's questions. That first 5 minutes help to relax the candidate and get him or her excited about the job. Part of the process is "selling" the candidate on the job, of course!

Do not exceed 30 minutes. In other words, stick to that 5-20-5 rule. Yes, this is redundant, but it's important! The phone screen exists to make the process more efficient, not less; so if you're spending more than 30 minutes, you need to speak more concisely and choose your questions more carefully.

Be prepared to pass. If you are indecisive and would feel uncomfortable terminating a candidacy unilaterally, you should not be conducting phone screens. Instead, ask a co-worker to do it or have a co-worker on the call with you to "train" you. By the end of the 30 minutes, you should have a clear idea in your head about whether or not to proceed.

Standardizing the questions is especially important for cases where several people are interviewing different candidates. To further ensure consistency, organize your questions by level of difficulty. The questions should be specific to the job, of course. This doesn't mean you have to ask all the questions or cannot deviate from the questions during the call, but for an appropriate baseline, at least, some of the standardized questions should be asked.

Test the questions. Ask co-workers who already hold the targeted job—or a similar one—the questions. You may be surprised to learn that the questions are too hard, or better left to an on-site setting with a whiteboard nearby. Vetting the questions before a phone screen will also give you confidence. If the candidate falters, you'll know whether it's because the question is difficult or because the candidate lacks a critical skill.

Go in prepared; know the candidate. Review the candidate's resume (and portfolio, if applicable) before the interview. A quick Google or social network search may be useful. Use this prep to focus the discussion. Make sure you ask the subset of standardized questions that verify some of the claims on the person's resume.

Write down your thoughts during (or immediately after) the call. The paper trail will help you communicate the results to others. The feedback will (ideally) help them improve the candidate pool over time. Don't wait until later, when your memory of the conversation will be less vivid. Come up with a standard form that you and others can use to record your thoughts. Include key points such as technical competence (score of 1–5, with optional comments), communication skills (1–5), engagement (1–5), and experience or skills (1–5).

End on a positive note. If you are optimistic about the candidate and would like him to move forward in the process, let him know. If you aren't excited about his or her prospects with your company, end by thanking the candidate and tell them that someone in HR will be contacting them within two days if they have been selected for an onsite interview.

Remember, don't feel obligated to give them a second interview immediately even if you're positive you'd like to meet them in person. The best practice is to end the conversation with, "We'll be in touch in two days."

Never share your interview questions with recruiters. While often well-intentioned, I've found recruiters tend to tip off the candidates if given the chance. Their incentives, after all, are based on these people getting hired! Do not tell a recruiter that a candidate couldn't read a balance sheet, for example; just indicate that the candidate did not meet the minimum level of technical proficiency.

CHAPTER 22
Don't Ask These Questions!

Don't Ask these Questions!

It never fails. At some point during the interview, the manager says, "So, why are manhole covers round?" or "If you could be an animal, what would you be and why?"

When I review my clients' interview questions, I first look for irrelevant or pointless ones. They are the first to go. Does the question "Why are manhole covers round?" or "If you were an animal, what would you be?" help you determine if a candidate is a fit the culture of the company or functions required by the job? Of course not. Yet, I see these types of questions again and again. Some individuals read about it on the internet, or maybe they think it makes them sound clever or smart. Whatever the case, they don't work. So, let's eliminate them because they don't belong. Here's why:

- They waste time (yours and the candidates).
- They are patronizing and condescending, especially to professionals.
- They make the interviewer look silly or unprofessional.
- Candidates know most of them and already have a "canned" answer.
- You will alienate your best candidates.

By the way, manhole covers are round because they require less material than square ones, they can be placed over the manhole easily without aligning them, and it's easier to move a 150-pound cover by rolling it.

Sadly, some of the biggest corporations still have these irrelevant questions listed in their interview playbooks. I know because I have seen them firsthand. Glassdoor.com compiled the top 25 oddball questions from thousands of interviews with candidates who provided them. Here they are:

DON'T ASK THESE QUESTIONS!

1. *"If you could throw a parade through the Zappos office, what type of parade would it be?"* Zappos

2. *If you could be any superhero, who would it be?"* AT&T

3. *"If you were a tree, which tree would you be?"* First Data

4. *If you could be any animal, what would you be and why?* Pacific Sunwear

5. *"If you could be shrunk to the size of a pencil and put in a blender, how would you get out?"* Goldman Sachs

6. *"What would you do if you just inherited a pizzeria from your uncle?"* Volkswagen

7. *"What would you do if you were the one survivor in a plane crash?"* Airbnb

8. *"Who would win in a fight between Spiderman and Batman?"* Stanford University

9. *"If both a taxi and a limo are priced the same, which one would you choose?"* Best Buy

10. *"Describe the color yellow to somebody who's blind."* Spirit Airlines

11. *"How many tennis balls are in this room and why?"* Yahoo

12. *"If you were a brick in a wall, which brick would you be and why?* Nestle USA

13. *"Are your parents disappointed with your career aspirations?"* Fisher Investments

14. *How many hair salons are there in Japan?* Boston Consulting

15. *Why are tennis balls fuzzy?* Nike

16. *How do you measure 9 minutes using only a 4-minute and 7-minute hourglass?* Bank of America

17. *"How many people are using Facebook in San Francisco at 2:30 pm on a Friday?"* Google

18. *"If Germans were the tallest people in the world, how would you prove it?"* Hewlett-Packard

19. *"How much money did residents of Dallas/Ft. Worth spend on gasoline in 2008?"* American Airlines

20. *"How many planes are currently flying over Kansas?"* Best Buy

21. *"Rate yourself on a scale of 1 to 10 how weird you are."* Capital One.

22. *"What is the philosophy of martial arts?"* Aflac.

23. *"How do you weigh an elephant without using a scale?"* IBM.

24. *"How are M&M's made?"* US Bank.

25. *"If you were asked to unload a 747 full of jelly beans, what would you do?"* Bose.

CHAPTER 23
The Top 30 Overused Interview Questions

The Top 30 Overused Interview Questions

Many of the questions below are standard interview questions that appear on the internet, books on acing the interview, career counselors, and the like. As such, the candidate has seen them as well and be sure they have prepared (canned) answers in response to them. I recommend that you stay away from them especially numbers one through five. The candidate is waiting for you to ask the question so they can dazzle you with their answer!

1. Tell me a little about yourself?

2. What is your greatest strength?

3. What is your greatest weakness?

4. How would you describe yourself?

5. What can you do for this company?

6. How did you hear about the position?

7. What do you know about the company?

8. Why do you want this job?

THE TOP 30 OVERUSED INTERVIEW QUESTIONS

9. Why should we hire you?

10. What is your greatest professional achievement?

11. Tell me about a challenge or conflict you've faced at work, and how you dealt with it.

12. What's your dream job?

13. What other companies are you interviewing?

14. Why are you leaving your current job?

15. What are you looking for in a new position?

16. What type of work environment do you prefer?

17. Are you the best person for this job? Why?

18. What can you contribute to this company?

19. What are your salary requirements?

20. What interests you about this job?

21. Describe your career goals.

22. Give some examples of teamwork.

23. How would you handle it if your boss was wrong?

24. If we asked people who knew you well why we should hire you, what would they say?

25. Is there a type of work environment you prefer?

26. What are your goals for the future?

27. What challenges are you looking for in your next job?

28. What did you like or dislike about your previous job?

29. What major challenges have you handled?

30. What was most or least rewarding about your job?

CHAPTER 24

Questions the Candidate May Ask

Questions the Candidate May Ask

Be prepared: Great candidates will interview <u>you</u>. They're not here begging for any old job; they want your company to be the perfect fit, and the right questions give them insights into the quality of your organization. Some interviewers may be put off by the questions below but understand this: Quality people won't work just anywhere. They are very selective (and can afford to be) about where they work, who they will be working for, and who they work with.

When addressing these questions, be sure to be honest, or it will come back to haunt you. The worst thing you can do is to sugarcoat the truth. The candidate will perceive it as lying. Worse, if they find out what you said was untrue after they began the job, they will never trust you or the company again.

Question number one is always on the candidate's mind, so mention it right up front—don't make them ask! Here's what you can expect:

1. Is this a new position? If not, what happened to the person who previously held this position?

2. What are the three or four most important factors that you consider when evaluating a promotion or pay raise?

3. How quickly can I move up in the company?

4. What are the common attributes of your top performers?

5. Will I be on a "fast track" for moving up in the company? If not, then why not?

QUESTIONS THE CANDIDATE MAY ASK

6. Can you tell me about someone in this position who did a terrific job, and what made it so terrific?

7. What is your vision of this job, and in your mind, what are the key responsibilities?

8. What are the biggest challenges that go with this position?

9. What is the turnover rate company-wide and for this and similar positions?

10. Is your company or department facing any major challenges?

11. Considering the people in your department or company, tell me how your most valued employees worked. What are the three to five things you believe makes them the most successful?

12. Explain your corporate culture and what type of person best fits into your organization.

13. What is your management style and what traits best match with your personality to create the most productive working environment?

14. During the first year, what are the key contributions you would expect from my performance?

15. What do you see as my greatest strengths for this position?

16. Tell me about the growth plans for the company.

17. In three to five years, where do you see my career going and what, specifically, should I do to get there?

18. Now that you've gotten to know me, how do you see my background adding value to your company?

19. What do you expect me to accomplish in the first 60 to 90 days?

20. What are the common attributes of your top performers?

21. What are your plans for increasing market share?

22. What is the most compelling reason to join your company?

23. Can I meet some of my potential team members?

24. What is your favorite part about working here?

25. Do you see any reason I might not be a good fit for this position?"

CHAPTER 25
Steering Clear of the EEOC

Steering Clear of the EEOC

Why do companies run afoul of the Equal Employment Opportunity Commission's (EEOC) rules? The reasons are varied, and most companies do not mean to break the law. An inexperienced interviewer may not have been trained properly, for example. Many hiring managers use questions about family as an icebreaker for interviews, not realizing that innocent inquiries about a spouse, children, etc., are unlawful. Employers ask too many questions in the interview that may get them in trouble. Even experienced managers will ask an awkward (and illegal) question without knowing that they are breaking the law.

Most job seekers don't want to sue over these practices. They just don't want to be in a position when their religion, lifestyle or heritage gets in the way of an even chance of being hired. Be aware that some people will file a complaint because they are overly sensitive about their age, religion or disability. Each state makes it easy to make fill out an online complaint. Once started, it will be the beginning of a long and expensive process (whether you are guilty or not). However, if the employer states questions so that they directly relate to specific occupational qualifications, then the questions may be legitimate. Clearly, the intent behind the question needs to be examined. Here's a great piece of advice: When in doubt, leave it out.

I experienced a situation firsthand when we were conducting phone interviews for an administrative position within my company. I received a letter from the EEOC regarding discriminatory practices. A woman we interviewed (and did not hire) claimed she didn't get the job because of her color, religion, age, and gender. She covered all the bases. But why should she want to sue a small consulting company?

I made a call to the EEOC and discovered that she thought she was applying for a job at Pinnacle Health Systems. I explained to the agent that her accusations were false and despite the fact that I didn't meet the EEOC guidelines (under 15 employees) I then had to prove I wasn't Pinnacle Health Systems AND that I had fewer than 15 employees.

I had to provide five years of payroll records, articles of incorporation, and my employer identification number (EIN). After several months, the agent was satisfied and dropped the case. Before we ended the call, she mentioned that I would be getting a letter from the Pennsylvania Human Relations Agency (if I hadn't received one already). Whenever the EEOC takes an action against an employer, the Pennsylvania Human Relations Commission is automatically notified. A month later, the PHRC contacted me, and the whole process was repeated!

Before asking a "delicate" (possibly illegal) question, consider what is the intent of asking? Will it get in the way of the candidate doing their job successfully? Will it put an undue strain on their family? Do they run the risk of a having an accident on the job? Here is a list of illegal questions and recommended legal ones.

Note: At the time of this writing, the information contained in this chapter is accurate, however, Federal and state guidelines may change. Seek the advice of a professional if you are unsure as to the legality of your question.

Nationality

It's illegal to ask a job seeker about their nationality, citizenship status, native language, or how long they have lived in the U.S. You can ask, however, if they are legally able to work in the United States.

Examples:

    What's your nationality?

    Is English your first language?

    Would working with people of another race (or religion) be a problem? We are a Christian (or Jewish or Muslim) company. Do you think you would be happy working here?

Are your parents from another country?

What was your first language?

What languages do your parents speak?

Are you bilingual?

What's the origin of your name?

What language do you speak at home?

That's an interesting accent. Where were you born?

What was your first language?

Religion:
It's not permissible to ask what religion job seekers practice, what religious holidays they observe, or their religious affiliations.

Examples:

What religious holidays do you practice?

Is there any day of the week you're not able to work?

Do you belong to a church?

Do you sing in a church choir?

Do your children go to Sunday school?

What do you do on Sundays?

Are you active in your church?

Are you a member of any religious group?

Are you "born-again?"

Are there any days you cannot work because of your religion?

Finances:

You cannot ask about current or past assets, liabilities, credit rating, bankruptcy or garnishment, refusal or cancelation of bonding, car ownership, rental or ownership of a house, the length of residence at an address, charge accounts or bank accounts.

Examples:
- What's your economic status?
- What kind of car do you drive?
- Who paid for your education?
- Do you have any outstanding debt?
- Do you own or rent your home?
- If you rent your home, are you planning to own your home in the future?
- Do you have a life insurance policy?
- How much insurance do you have?
- What is your net worth?

Age:

Do not ask any questions about age beyond asking if they are 18 years or older. The Age Discrimination in Employment Act of 1967 (ADEA) protects individuals who are 40 years of age or older from employment discrimination based on age. Asking something job specific is acceptable—"Are you eligible to serve alcohol?" is permitted.

Examples:
- How old are you?
- When were you born?
- When were you married?
- How old are your children?

When did you graduate from high school?

When did you graduate from college?

There is a large disparity between your age and that of your co-workers. Is this a problem for you?

Marital and family status:
While it's permissible for interviewers to ask whether you have ever used another name in work or academic situations, it's illegal to ask questions about your maiden name or marital status.

Examples:
- Does your wife work?
- Do you live with someone?
- When are you planning on having children?
- Does your husband work?
- Who takes care of your children while you're at work?
- How many children do you have?
- Are you married, single or divorced?
- Do you consider yourself to be a family man (woman)?
- Do you intend to get married soon?
- Do you have children?
- Are you a single parent?
- What are your long-range plans for a family?
- How many people live in your household?
- Do you live by yourself?
- Do you have someone who takes care of a sick child?
- What does your spouse think about your career?

Gender:

It is illegal to ask questions relating to the individual's gender, sexual preference or lifestyle questions relating to gender.

Examples:
> What's your sexual orientation?
>
> Are you a member of any gay or lesbian groups?
>
> Are you straight?
>
> Do you date members of the opposite or same sex?

Health and physical abilities:

It's illegal to ask job seekers if they smoke, drink or take drugs. Questions about height, weight, use of sick days, the presence of disabilities or past operations/sicknesses are similarly off limits. Interviewers do have the right to ask if you've violated company policies regarding alcohol or tobacco, whether you use illegal drugs (as opposed to simply "drugs"). They can also ask if you're able to lift a given weight or reach items on shelves that are at a particular height, how many workdays you missed in the past year, whether you're physically capable of executing the position's specific duties. In other words, whether or not you can perform the job with or without reasonable accommodations.

Examples
> Have you experienced any serious illnesses in the past year?
>
> How did you get that scar/mark/limp/other physical abnormality?
>
> Have you ever been turned down for a life insurance policy?
>
> How well is your hearing?
>
> Do you have any preexisting health issues that might impact our health insurance plan?
>
> Have you ever been hospitalized?

Have you ever taken a stress test?

Do you have any disabilities?

Is anyone in your family disabled?

Have you ever been addicted to drugs?

Have you ever filed for workers' compensation?

Do you see a physician on a regular basis?

When was your last medical checkup?

Do you have large prescription drug bills?

Residence:

It is illegal to ask how far away a job seeker lives, but it's permissible to ask if the candidate can start work at a given hour or if he is willing to relocate.

Examples

Where do you live?

Do you live more than an hours' drive from here?

What state do you have your driver's license?

Are you planning to move out of area?

Criminal record:

Human resource professionals agree that asking an applicant about their criminal history is difficult. Below are a few guidelines to consider.

As an employer you can ask the applicant questions about any criminal convictions he has received. A conviction means the job applicant was found guilty after a trial or pleaded guilty to a crime in exchange for a lighter sentence. You can ask about the type of conviction and the date of the conviction, along with the successful completion of all sentencing requirements, such as probation.

Arrests

Some states, including North Dakota, do not allow an interviewer to ask questions about criminal arrests. Others, such as New Jersey, have no laws preventing you from asking questions about an arrest. A criminal arrest can be for a felony or a misdemeanor offense and involves a case in which a criminal charge was filed but not pursued by the district attorney's office. Questions to ask should involve the year of the occurrence, the type of case and any details that might bear on the position.

Military service:

It is illegal for an employer to discriminate against a member of the Armed Forces, National Guard or Reserves, but it is legal to ask if the job seeker anticipates requiring extended time away from work.

Examples

    How long did you serve in the Army?

    What type of discharge did you receive in the military?

    How often are you deployed for your Army Reserve training exercises?

Miscellaneous Unacceptable Personal Questions:

    Are you comfortable working for a female boss?

    Are you accident prone?

    How long do you plan to work until you retire?

    Do you drink socially?

    Where did you live while you were growing up?

    How much do you weigh?

    What organizations do you belong to?

    Are you a registered Republican/Democrat/other?

Who did you vote for in the last election?

When was the last time you had a car accident?

What ties do you have to your community?

How do you contribute to the community?

Are you living with anyone?

How tall are you?

What charities do you support?

Do you think you can work for a younger person?

Do you consider yourself to be a social drinker?

When was the last time you used illegal drugs?